PRAISE FOR PAUL KRASSNER

"Thanks to Paul Krassner for continuing to be the lobster claw in the tuna casserole of modern America."
—Tom Robbins

"The FBI was right; this man is dangerous—and funny, and necessary."
—George Carlin

"Krassner is one of the best minds of his generation to be destroyed by madness, starving, hysterical, naked—but mainly hysterical."
—Art Spiegelman

"I have been a fan of his since I was a snot-nosed kid, and his words have been a driving force and influence on my life. . . . If you have read his work before, you know the joys that you are in for. If you haven't, start reading, and consider this your lucky day. For Paul Krassner is an activist, a philosopher, a lunatic and a saint, but most of all he is funny."
—Lewis Black

"Paul taught me that extreme stylistic accuracy could make even the most bizarre comedic concept credible. . . . He is a unique character on the American landscape. A self-described 'investigative satirist,' he straddles the lines between politics, culture, pornography and drugs—in other words, the land where all of us, were we really honest with ourselves, would choose to dwell."
—Harry Shearer

"Krassner loves ironies, especially stinging ironies that nettle public figures. He would rather savor a piquant irony about a public figure than eat a bowl of fresh strawberries and ice cream."
—Ken Kesey

"Krassner is absolutely compelling. He has lived on the edge so long he gets his mail delivered there."
—*San Francisco Chronicle*

"He is an expert at ferreting out hypocrisy and absurdism from the more solemn crannies of American culture."
—*New York Times*

"Krassner has the uncanny ability to alter your perceptions permanently."
—*Los Angeles Times*

"I told Krassner one time that his writings made me hopeful. He found this an odd compliment to offer a satirist. I explained that he made supposedly serious matters seem ridiculous, and that this inspired many of his readers to decide for themselves what was ridiculous and what was not. Knowing that there were people doing that, better late than never, made me optimistic."
—Kurt Vonnegut

WHO'S TO SAY
WHAT'S OBSCENE?

How a Satirical Editor Became a Yippie Conspirator in Ten Easy Years

Best of The Realist EDITOR

Confessions of a Raving Unconfined Nut: Misadventures in the Counterculture

The Winner of the Slow Bicycle Race: The Satirical Writings of Paul Krassner

Sex, Drugs and the Twinkie Murders: 40 Years of Countercultural Journalism

Impolite Interviews

Pot Stories for the Soul EDITOR

Psychedelic Trips for the Mind EDITOR

Magic Mushrooms and Other Highs: From Toad Slime to Ecstasy EDITOR

Murder at the Conspiracy Convention and Other American Absurdities

One Hand Jerking: Reports From an Investigative Satirist

Tales of Tongue Fu

In Praise of Indecency: Dispatches From the Valley of Porn

WHO'S TO SAY WHAT'S OBSCENE?

Politics, Culture and Comedy in America Today

PAUL KRASSNER

Foreword by Arianna Huffington

City Lights Books • San Francisco

All the pieces in this book were originally published in *High Times*, *AVN Online*, *Season in the Sun*, *Huffington Post*, *Counterpunch*, *Reality Sandwich* and *ArthurMag.com*—except for the following: "Fear and Laughing in Las Vegas" and "Strange Bedfellows Among the Yippies" were published in *The Nation*. "Great Moments in Memory Loss" was published in the *New York Press*. A shorter version of "Who's to Say What's Obscene?" was published in *Funny Times*. A shorter version of "The Disneyland Memorial Orgy" was published in the *LA Weekly*. A shorter version of "The Parts Left Out of *Chicago 10*" was published in the *Los Angeles Times*.

Cover design: Pollen

Cover image: Wally Wood, "The Disneyland Memorial Orgy," Copyright © 2006 by Paul Krassner.

Library of Congress Cataloging-in-Publication Data

Krassner, Paul.
Who's to say what's obscene : politics, culture and comedy in America today / by Paul Krassner ; foreword by Arianna Huffington.
    p. cm.
  ISBN 978-0-87286-501-3
  1. Satire, American. I. Title.
  PS3561.R286W47 2009
  814'.54—dc22
                        2009002813

City Lights Books are published at the City Lights Bookstore, 261 Columbus Avenue, San Francisco, CA 94133.
www.citylights.com

CONTENTS

Foreword by Arianna Huffington *xi*

I. WE HAVE WAYS OF MAKING YOU LAUGH *1*
Who's to Say What's Obscene? *1*
Mort Sahl's Best Punch Line *18*
Barbarian at the Gate *24*
Fear and Laughing in Las Vegas *29*
Don Imus Meets Michael Richards *35*
The Great Muhammad Cartoon Controversy *51*
The Disneyland Memorial Orgy *56*
The Parts Left Out of *Borat* *63*
Getting High Down Under *69*
Harry Shearer Hears Voices *73*
The Power of Laughter *77*

II. THE WAR ON SOME PEOPLE WHO USE SOME DRUGS *81*
The Ballad of Tommy Chong *81*
Barack Obama and the Pot Laws *85*
Bong Hits 4 Jesus *88*
Was Moses Tripping? *93*
Hookahs on Parade *96*
Got Vomit? *99*
How Magic Are Your Mushrooms? *102*

III. UNDER THE COUNTERCULTURE *107*
Hippies on the Hitler Channel *107*
Strange Bedfellows Among the Yippies *112*

The Parts Left Out of *Chicago 10* 116
The Grateful Dead Play the Pyramids 127

IV. SEVERAL DEAD ICONS *131*

Ginsberg's Last Laugh *131*
Robert Anton Wilson: Keep the Lasagna Flying! *139*
Who the Hell Is Stew Albert? *143*
Kurt Vonnegut Lives! *145*
Peter Stafford Meets Tom Snyder *150*
Albert Ellis Meets Lenny Bruce *153*
Norman Mailer's Foreskin *157*
Mountain Girl Remembers Albert
        Hofmann *160*
Michael Rossman: A Touch of Sativa *163*
George Carlin Has Left the Green Room *171*

V. FREEDOM'S JUST ANOTHER WORD *177*

Exclusive Interview with Michael Phelps *177*
There Are No Atheists in the White House *179*
Great Moments in Memory Loss *193*
Trashing the Right to Read *200*
The Thought Police at Work *206*
Donuts, Coffee and Weed *213*
Welcome to Camp Mogul *216*
Campaign in the Ass *219*
Behind the Infamous Twinkie Defense *222*
The Last Election *233*
And God Said, "Let There Be FILF" *237*

About the author *241*

For Nancy, my constant muse

"Satire is a sort of glass, wherein beholders do
generally discover everybody's face but their own."
—Jonathan Swift

FOREWORD BY ARIANNA HUFFINGTON

Eight years after 9/11, eight years after Ari Fleischer warned Americans that they "need to watch what they say, watch what they do," eight years after Graydon Carter declared the death of the age of irony, eight years after *Politically Incorrect* was pushed off the air, and 280 years after Jonathan Swift made his *Modest Proposal* that Irish children be sold as food, we seem to be living in a Golden Age of political humor—and especially political satire: Jon Stewart, Bill Maher, Stephen Colbert, viral YouTube videos, and after thirty-three years on the air, the rebirth of *Saturday Night Live*, which went from "Is that still on?" to MustSeeTV (or at least Must See on YouTube).

They are all standing on the shoulders of the great comedic bomb-throwers of the past: Lenny Bruce, Richard Pryor, George Carlin, the Smothers Brothers, the gang at *National Lampoon*.

And Paul Krassner—confidant of Lenny, cofounder of the Yippies, defiler of Disney characters, publisher of *The Realist*, investigative satirist extraordinaire.

As soon as we decided to create the *Huffington Post*, I knew I wanted Paul Krassner involved. His irreverence was just what the blog doctor ordered. He posted three times during the week we launched and has been at it ever since. One hundred fifty-seven posts and counting. But who's counting?

For the longest time, American humor had lost its bite. Punch lines with a purpose, satire in the tradition of Jonathan Swift, savage wit at the service of passionate conviction had given way to the domesticated yucks of sitcoms, late-night jokes and official Washington dinners where politicians and the media skewer each other in harmless ritual combat without any fear that things might be different in the morning (Stephen Colbert's legendary scorched-earth performance at the White House correspondents' dinner in 2006 was the exception; Rich Little's painfully bad 2007 follow-up the rule).

All the while, Krassner was toiling away, tilling the comedy soil and planting the subversive seeds that would flower into the bumper crop of satire we are harvesting today.

Katie Couric's multipart interview with Sarah Palin was the turning point in how the country saw Palin—and by extension John McCain. But it was Tina Fey's pitch-perfect take on Palin, replayed endlessly on YouTube (and *HuffPost*) and spread virally online, that delivered the coup de grace. It was a comedy mugging for the ages.

Jon Stewart is now the most trusted name in news for the Facebook set. Stephen Colbert's "truthiness" perfectly defined the Bush administration's denigration of facts. *South Park* and *Family Guy* routinely draw blood with drawn characters. *Doonesbury* still regularly delivers a knockout punch.

And Paul Krassner keeps delivering incendiary

journalism. This collection includes some of his best. Don't miss the bit on Palin Porn ("No anal required").

Lewis Lapham identified the satirist's work as "the crime of arson, meaning to set a torch of words to the hospitality tents of the pompous and self-righteous." And that great satiric arsonist Mark Twain wrote that exposure to good satire makes citizens less likely to be, as he put it, "shriveled into sheep."

The great satirists have always been passionate reformers challenging the status quo. I once called Paul for a column I was writing and asked him how he saw his job. "Sometimes," he told me, "humor is just a way of calling attention to the contradictions or the hypocrisy that's going on officially. That's the function of humor—it can alter your reality."

Krassner has been altering our reality for some fifty years. In the process, he has inspired the work of many—including John Cusack, who says that Krassner's radical approach to truth-telling informed his film *War, Inc.*—a savage, reality-altering take on Iraq.

When, in 1729, Jonathan Swift wrote *A Modest Proposal*, he was seeking to turn a spotlight on the indifference toward the twin Irish crises of overpopulation and hunger. His proposal was to feed young children to hungry men. "I have been assured," he wrote, "that a young healthy child, well-nursed, is at a year old a most delicious, nourishing, and wholesome food, whether stewed, roasted, baked or broiled; and I make no doubt in that it will equally serve in a fricassee or a ragout."

In this book, Krassner carries on that savory tradition.

Read it and laugh. And wince. And become outraged. And laugh some more.

1.

WE HAVE WAYS OF MAKING YOU LAUGH

WHO'S TO SAY WHAT'S OBSCENE?

I'm not talking about profanity or pornography here.

Take, for example, the fact that Barack Obama's chief of staff backed immunity for those in the Bush administration who were the architects of justification for torture and indefinite detention without trial. Now *that's* fucking obscene. Fortunately for democracy, next day the president passed that decision on to the Department of Justice, but then not on to an independent investigation, where it belongs. I'm saddened and outraged by the lack of accountability in government agencies, multinational corporations and organized religions. Nobody takes responsibility for the anguish they cause unless they're prosecuted. Dehumanization's the name of the game, and its players reek with arrogance.

The creator of a new Coney Island sideshow attraction—the Waterboard Thrill Ride—asked a rhetorical question: "What's more obscene, the official position that waterboarding is not torture, or our official position that it's a thrill ride?"

Tom Hayden wrote in an op-ed piece: "With the Congress including $50 million for the arts in the economic package, the overall annual budget for the NEA will be just short of $200 million for the coming year. By comparison we spend more on the Iraq War every day, or $341.4 million, according to the Web site *costofwar.com*. This is the real obscenity that goes uncensored. Yet funding for the arts is more controversial than funding for war. For decades, arts subsidies have been targeted as frivolous waste by many of the same conservative Republicans willing to budget trillions for the wars in Iraq and Afghanistan."

In a letter to the editor of the *Los Angeles Times*, Ken Johnson stated: "It's fine to demand that U.S. automakers seeking federal money meet higher mileage requirements. But what about the workers who would pay for this increase in efficiency with their jobs? It's obscene that these corporate incompetents are begging for more of our tax dollars while at the same time contemplating more layoffs. It is even more obscene that our tough-talking lawmakers in Washington have said nothing about insisting that taxpayer money be used first to preserve these jobs. To give these automakers untold numbers of dollars while allowing them to then place thousands of skilled people on the public dole is just plain sinful."

A syndicated editorial cartoon by Jeff Parker depicted a job-seeker at the unemployment office explaining to the jaded clerk, "I'm looking for a high-powered executive position where I can wreck the company and still get an obscene, bailout-funded bonus . . . y'know, like those guys at A.I.G."

It's obscene that a secret state police report describes supporters of presidential candidates Ron Paul, Chuck Baldwin and Bob Barr as militia-influenced terrorists and instructs the Missouri police to be on the lookout for the display of bumper stickers and other paraphernalia associated with the Constitutional, Campaign for Liberty, and Libertarian parties. This ain't creeping fascism, it's galloping fascism.

It's obscene that former Vice President Dick Cheney's office deleted nearly half of congressional testimony about the consequences of climate change on public health. The vast profits of our current energy, health care, insurance, pharmaceutical and credit-lending industries—all utterly obscene.

Even the notion that Starbucks can actually offer customers up to 87,000 drink combinations is obscene. Stephen Colbert—as if responding to the ability of Comcast, the country's largest cable company, to provide a thousand channels—coined a phrase, "the obscene cult of superficiality."

A recent book by Rick Wartzman is titled *Obscene in the Extreme: The Burning and Banning of John Steinbeck's The Grapes of Wrath*. California Deputy Attorney General Zackery Morazzini argues that the U.S. Supreme Court has already limited children's access to sexually explicit material and that "violent video games are just as obscene." Conversely, when Facebook removed from its Web site photos of women nursing their babies, "lactivists" in cyberspace formed a group of more than 100,000 called "Hey, Facebook, Breastfeeding Is Not Obscene."

There's a trickle-down effect of morally obscene behavior in process: from those officials who approved international torture, down to the brutality permitted in the U.S. prison system; from Karl Rove refusing to testify under oath about the political firing of several U.S. attorneys, down to our court system itself, where a recently released African American spent twenty-six years of his life behind bars because the prosecutors violated their professional duty by holding back evidence of his innocence. And yet they cannot be legally punished for it. At the very least, force 'em to be given empathy implants.

◆ ◆ ◆

Irreverence is my only sacred cow, and the more repression there is, the more need there is for irreverence toward those who are responsible for that repression. But these days, sarcasm passes for irony. Name-calling passes for insight. Bleeped-out four-letter words pass for wit. Easy-reference jokes pass for analysis, and the audience applauds itself for recognizing the reference.

So many jokes that are based on looks and gaffes tend to trivialize them all. Good satire should have a point of view. It doesn't have to get a belly laugh, it just has to be valid criticism, which is the classic definition of satire. Jokes with no meaningful point of view aim for the lowest common denominator, along with commercials for erectile dysfunction and politicians alike. During the 2008 presidential campaign, candidates made 110 guest shots on late-night TV shows, up from twenty-five in 2004. The appearance of political candidates on comedy shows is intended to humanize them for voters.

That's why in 1968 Richard Nixon said "Sock it to me" on *Laugh-In* and why his opponent Hubert Humphrey regretted turning down their invitation to say it. Why forty years later Jay Leno tosses softball questions to such guests. Why David Letterman's writers supplied Hillary Clinton with a "Top Ten" list to read off the teleprompter. Why politicians go on *The Daily Show* so that Jon Stewart can interrupt their mini stump speeches with his own compulsive punch lines. When the Pew Research Center asked Americans to name the journalist they most admired, they placed Stewart at number four, tied with Tom Brokaw, Dan Rather and Anderson Cooper.

Ironically, a local news channel in Los Angeles has been a sponsor of *The Colbert Report*. Yes, a real news show advertising on a fake news show. When Colbert was asked what he finds to be most shocking, he said, "People mistaking me for real news." Of course, people make the same mistake about Fox News. In July 2007, a school administrator sued Fox because he was ridiculed and harassed after a fake news story—buttressed by the anchors assuring viewers they were "not making this up"—repeated a Web site prank claiming that he had suspended a pupil for tossing a ham bone on a table occupied by Somali students, knowing that the Muslims would be offended, then said, "These children have got to learn that ham is not a toy," and that there was an effort to create an "anti-ham response plan."

Just to make people laugh is fine, yet one wonders if the late–night TV talk-show monologues actually help to pacify the audience—what Herbert Marcuse called "repressive tolerance." But Conan O'Brien's job is to entertain his viewers, not to mobilize them. And what would a comedian mobilize an audience to *do*? Andy Kaufman mobilized his audience to go out and join him for milk and cookies. Stephen Colbert mobilized his audience to go out and buy his book. Bill Maher mobilized his audience to go out and see his movie.

Maher entertains and impacts the consciousness of his audiences, yet it was also because of his material and/or his support of Barack Obama and/or his docucomedy *Religulous* that a package with a threatening letter and suspicious white powder was addressed to him and opened by a staffer at the McCallum Theater in Palm Desert, California, on a Friday in October, 2008. Authorities rushed a hazardous materials team to the theater, which was shut down and quarantined for five hours. Four employees who came into contact with the package were decontaminated, and the others were evacuated. Singer/guitarist Boz Scaggs's concert that night was canceled.

Field testing indicated that the powder wasn't harmful. Maher had been scheduled to appear on Saturday night, and perform he did, though ticket holders had to pass through a metal detector after depositing their keys, cell phones and other electronic devices into a basket. Maher didn't mention the incident during his act, but as he walked off the stage at the end of his show, he said to the audience, "Sorry for the trouble." On the same day that the package for him was delivered to the theater, a similar one was received at the *Los Angeles Times*, addressed to two reporters. Written on the envelope inside was "Save the Babies" and "Kill All Obama Supporters." The previous day, a similar package was delivered to an Obama campaign office in Los Angeles.

Although occasionally a viewer of Maher's program will tell him of being "turned around" politically, in the wishful-thinking corner of my mind, pushing comedic limits and fostering social change would be inextricably connected. People don't like to be lectured at, but if you can make them laugh, their defenses are down, and if there's a truth embedded in that humor, they've accepted it for the moment by laughing. And when there's a large audience, no matter how disparate their background, if they're laughing together, it's a unifying moment. But who knows how long that moment of truth or insight will last, for how many members of the audience, and whether knowing it will lead to any action? It's just one more bit of input, hardly a tipping point.

Besides, the truth is Silly Putty. With the advent of Photoshop and the ability to alter images imperceptibly, the maxim "Pictures don't lie" can now be buried in the Outdated Metaphors Graveyard, along with "That's like bringing coals to Newcastle" (they finally ran out of coal), and "As good as gold" (for all we know, Fort Knox is currently filled with stacks of Shredded Wheat).

When Rolling Stones guitarist Keith Richards told a reporter that he had snorted his father's ashes mixed with cocaine, I believed him. But when he claimed this was only an April Fool's joke, I believed that too. And when he later said that the real meaning of his statement was "lost in translation"—that he was merely trying to express "how tight" the relationship with his father had been—I also believed that. All three responses were possible. Even probable.

◆ ◆ ◆

Steve Allen once observed, "Comedy is tragedy plus time," but everything is accelerating. Even the rate of acceleration is accelerating. The time between tragedy and comedy gets shorter and shorter. The more news there is, the more victims there are to serve as set-ups for punch lines.

On the same day that people were being burned alive in the fire at the Branch Davidian compound in Waco, Texas, Jay Leno did a joke in his *Tonight Show* monologue about there being two kinds of cult members there—"regular and crispy."

(In January 2009, on the same day that a plane crashed into the Hudson River, Leno did jokes about it, but since nobody died, that rendered the accident more acceptable as a source of humor.)

In September 2008—on the same day that the stock market dove 500 points and Hurricane Ike devastated Texas—Stephen Colbert said, "Thank God I have my money stashed on a boat in Galveston."

In November—ten days after the election resulted in a revocation of the right to same-sex marriage in California, and *while* the fires in California were becoming increasingly catastrophic—Bill Maher, in his opening monologue on *Real Time*, acknowledged the seriousness of those spreading flames. I knew it was a straight line, and I cringed with curiosity as to what the punch line might be. "But the fires could've been much worse," said Maher. "Gay people could've been married."

In April 2009, while swine flu deaths were still occurring, Jon Stewart managed to find comedy in the possibly impending pandemic. If you host a daily satirical program, it becomes a matter of topicality *über alles*.

When it was first decided that a fence would be installed to prevent Mexicans from sneaking across the border into the United States, I was performing stand-up and announced that "the government is now hiring illegal immigrants to build a fence that will keep themselves out of this country." Some months later, in December 2006, the Golden State Fence Company in Southern California agreed to pay nearly $5 million in fines for hiring undocumented workers, and the company's work actually included constructing part of the fence separating Tijuana, Mexico, from San Diego, California.

That might seem like satirical prophecy, but reality has long been nipping at the heels of satire. In fact, during the past several years, with ever-increasing frequency, reality has been *outrunning* satire. It wasn't a comedian who said, "There was a pair of dinosaurs on Noah's Ark." It was a creationist sincerely trying to reconcile the disconnect between science and religion.

His unintentional joke became an actuality in 2007 at the Creationist Museum in Kentucky, funded for $27 million by evangelical Christians, which presents a Biblical version of history indicating that the universe is not 14 billion years old, but rather that God created Earth in six days 6,000 years ago, and that Cain married his sister in order to populate the planet. One room features two teenagers who were indoctrinated with evolution; the girl is talking to Planned Parenthood; the boy is looking at porn.

A satirist could also have come up with something as absurd as O.J. Simpson's book and television project, *If I Did It*, but one person's sense of humor is another person's entrepreneurial outlook. That multimedia fantasy was aborted by its own creators—Judith Regan, who came to fame when she handled Howard Stern's *Private Parts*, and Fox TV's Rupert Murdoch, who has struggled so diligently to give insensitivity a bad name—then resurrected by a different publisher in 2007 for the Goldman family as a way of getting some of Simpson's money awarded to them in the civil suit that found him guilty of a double murder. Simpson is presently in prison for murdering his memorabilia.

And, just as that little two-letter word, "if," might as well have been omitted from Simpson's title, John Kerry's accidental failure to *include* in a speech another little two-letter word—"us" as in "get *us* stuck in Iraq"—contributed to his downfall in the presidential campaign. The notion that he *meant* to insult the troops in Iraq became the party line of cheerleaders for the neocon propaganda team, deliberately misunderstanding what Kerry intended to say until he had to apologize with the same false humility that the lawyer who was shot by Dick Cheney apologized for allowing his face to get in the way of Cheney's shotgun.

A thirteen-letter wail of, ironically, confidence—"*Yeee-aaaggghhh!*"—knocked Howard Dean right out of the 2004 presidential race. A six-letter word, "macaca," not only deleted George Allen's presidential fantasy, it also enabled the Democrats to win the Senate in the 2006 midterm election with the vote for Allen's adversary, Jim Webb. There was even hope in Republican circles that Barack Obama's seven-letter middle name, Hussein, would spoil his chance of being elected president in 2008.

Dennis Miller stooped to making "short jokes" about Dennis Kucinich, who had the fortitude to call for the impeachment of Dick Cheney and George Bush while his colleagues continued to eat grilled chickenshit sandwiches for breakfast over the issue. That's one thing Nancy Pelosi *didn't* take off the table.

During one of the debates among Democratic candidates, the moment that the late Tim Russett said to Kucinich,

"This is a serious question," you knew it wouldn't be. A different journalist might have asked, "Why do think that Cheney should be impeached before Bush?" But Russert further marginalized Kucinich, ridiculing him in a flying saucer kind of way. Like a trial lawyer who already knows what a defendant's answer will be, his "serious question" was "Did you see a UFO?"

Kucinich tried to explain that the U in UFO means "unidentified" flying object. He joked, "I'm moving my campaign office to Roswell, New Mexico, and Exeter, New Hampshire." He pointed out that Jimmy Carter had seen a UFO. Russert interrupted him with a statistic: 14 percent of Americans have seen UFOs. Kucinich asked him to repeat that number, as if to thank him for inadvertently providing him with the UFO-sighters vote. Russert repeated the number, and then, with the smug satisfaction of having generated a guaranteed sound bite, he said, "I want to ask Senator Obama. . . ." Predictably, there was a trickle-down effect. The next day, I was asked if it was true that Kucinich had seen "some Martians."

Of course, there's a video of that interstellar encounter inside our secret government's implied-blackmail lockbox, along with the video of John McCain performing an abortion on Pat Robertson's mistress, and the video of a threesome—Charles Schumer, Dianne Feinstein and a billygoat—members of the Senate Judiciary Committee who voted to confirm Michael Mukasey as attorney general despite his refusal to say whether he felt waterboarding was torture. McCain passed the buck to the CIA—any torture they approve is good enough for him—despite the fact that he knows from personal experience that victims will tell torturers whatever they want to hear.

Brian Williams, in his capacity as a host of *Saturday Night Live*, referred to the mainstream media's assumption that Hillary Clinton would win in the primaries and then in the general election. From the perspective of the networks and cable channels: whoever. Since fundraising seems to be the essence of a political campaign, the candidate with the most money will buy the most TV commercials. And in the process, that old song "There's No Business Like Show Business," landed in the Outdated Sayings Graveyard, because there is indeed a business like show business. It's the news.

◆ ◆ ◆

In 1964, Lenny Bruce was found guilty of an "indecent performance" at the Cafe Au Go Go in Greenwich Village. In 2003, New York Governor George Pataki granted Bruce a posthumous pardon—but it was in the context of justifying the invasion of Iraq. "Freedom of speech is one of the great American liberties," Pataki said, "and I hope this pardon serves as a reminder of the precious freedoms we are fighting to preserve as we continue to wage the war on terrorism." Lenny would've felt exploited and bemused.

Earlier that year, when rock-star/activist Bono received an award at the Golden Globes ceremony, he said, "This is really, really fucking brilliant." The FCC ruled that he had not violated broadcast standards, because his use of the offending word was "unfortunate," but "isolated and non-sexual." You see, it was merely an "exclamative" adjective. The FCC did not consider Bono's utterance to be indecent because, in context, he obviously didn't use the word "fucking" to "describe sexual or excretory organs or activities."

But in 2004, during a duet with Janet Jackson, Justin Timberlake sang the lyric, "Gonna have you naked by the end of this song," and in what was defended as "a wardrobe malfunction," exposed her breast for .562 of a second during the halftime extravaganza at the Super Bowl. I had never seen the media make such a mountain out of an implant.

In 2007, a CBS lawyer argued unsuccessfully that the network should not be fined $550,000 for Jackson's breast-baring because it was fleeting, isolated and unauthorized. Still, that Nipplegate moment had provided a perfect excuse to crack down on indecency during an election year. So the FCC *reversed* their own decision, contending that Bono's utterance of "fucking brilliant" was "indecent and profane" after all. In 2008, an appeals court ruled that the FCC "acted arbitrarily and capriciously" in the Jackson case, and observed that the flashing of her breast happened too fast to be considered "so pervasive as to amount to 'shock treatment' for the audience." But then the FCC asked the Supreme Court to appeal that ruling.

At the live *Billboard Music Awards* show in 2002, Cher responded to her critics, "People have been telling me I'm on the way out every year, right? So fuck 'em. I still have a job and they don't." Next year on that same awards show, Nicole Richie recounted her *Simple Life* experience: "Have you ever tried to get cowshit out of a Prada purse? It's not so fucking simple." In both instances, the FCC ruled that Fox TV had violated their standards of decency because *any* use of the word "inherently has a sexual connotation." Each violation could result in a fine as high as $325,000.

An appeals court reversed the FCC's reversal in the Bono case, and suddenly he was, once again, not guilty of indecency. But, in April 2009—six days after Fox News anchor Shepard Smith shouted, "We are America! I don't give a rat's ass if it helps [get information from suspected terrorists]! We do not fucking torture!"—the Supreme Court upheld the FCC's ruling in the Cher/Richie case, and the reversal of Bono's reversal was reversed. It was suddenly retroactively unacceptable for him to say, "This is really, really fucking brilliant." And now, will former Governor Pataki revoke his posthumous pardon of Lenny Bruce?

◆ ◆ ◆

Sometimes it feels like I'm making up the news. Reality has become so bizarre that I seem to have lost the ability to tell the difference between truth and fiction. When columnist Rosa Brooks quoted former U.S. Ambassador to the U.N. John Bolton as saying, "I only hope the president has the good sense to bomb Iran before this diplomacy nonsense spreads any further," I thought he had really said that, but it was a satirical column. Conversely, when I heard that Mitt Romney was asked whether he would invade Iran if elected president, and he replied, "I'd have to ask my lawyers," I thought that was a made-up joke, but he really said it in earnest.

In December 2008, there was a report traveling around the Internet—with a fake Bloomberg News byline to encourage credibility—that Somali pirates, known for hijacking ships for ransom in the Gulf of Aden, were negotiating a purchase of Citigroup. I forwarded it to prolific humorist Andy Borowitz and asked, "Did you write this?" He replied, "No, but it's funny." A week later, Borowitz reported that while then-President-elect Obama continued "to assemble his 'team of rivals' by filling Cabinet positions with former political opponents, he has drawn the ire of one self-styled rival who feels he has been unfairly overlooked: Rep. Dennis Kucinich. . . . With most of the Cabinet posts having already gone to more prominent rivals such as Sen. Hillary Clinton and Gov. Bill Richardson, Mr. Kucinich's statements were widely seen as a Hail Mary bid to become Postmaster General."

A few people I forwarded that to thought it was literally true. One explained, "That was just for a moment. I forgot I was reading Andy Borowitz." I asked Borowitz if he could recall any other pseudo-journalistic reports he's posted that have had similar reactions.

"You know," he replied, "I've written so many columns that people have taken to be true, I don't know where to begin. I recently ended a piece with a bogus 'quote' from Doris Kearns Goodwin [author of *Team of Rivals*] which the *Kansas City Star* then attributed to her."

(Goodwin's quote—"Every time someone says 'team of rivals,' I sell another book on Amazon. Team of rivals, team of rivals, team of rivals"—had been preceded by this beginning: "Continuing in his quest to assemble a so-called 'team of rivals,' President-elect Barack Obama today announced that he would name Angelina Jolie and Jennifer Aniston to key Cabinet positions. The two actresses, who have been perennial tabloid fodder as a result of their longstanding feud over actor Brad Pitt, were surprise choices for Mr. Obama's Cabinet, since neither of them has been a government official or even portrayed one in a movie.")

"But," Borowitz continued, "this may be my favorite: During the primaries, when Hillary was trying to be all blue collar, she got Annie Oakley on us and claimed that she loved hunting as a little girl. I then wrote a piece about Dick Cheney challenging her to a hunting contest. The *Boston Herald* actually wrote an entire article about Cheney's challenge, without bothering to check who the source was."

Borowitz concluded, "Readers get confused by my articles all the time, but I love it when so-called journalists can't tell that they're made up."

When I was interviewed for a six-part PBS series, *Make 'Em Laugh: The Funny Business of America*, I mentioned—as an example of a dark reality that could be mistaken for dark humor—a widely criticized Dutch TV program that hoped to draw attention to a shortage of organ donors by having a terminally ill woman choose a contestant to receive one of her kidneys. The next day, the *Big Donor Show* was revealed as a hoax, with the producers explaining that they were trying to pressure the government into reforming organ donation laws.

At least their motivation had a certain idealism, as opposed to the motivation behind Fox TV's original intention to promote *If I Did It* during the November sweeps—a phenomenon comparable to *rumspringa*, the Amish tradition of "running-around time," when teenagers and young adult members of the plain-living Christian sect are allowed to act like their debauched non-Amish counterparts. The networks feature the raunchiest, most vulgar, most sensational, most violent, most gory, celebrity-laden programs they can produce, aiming much more than usual for the lowest possible common denominator in order to boost their ratings and charge higher rates for commercials. Potential sponsors buy into it every time, because we *viewers* are really the product being sold—to *them*.

Yet false piety continues to thrive. Senator Larry "I'm

not gay" Craig—whose opening statement at his August 2007 press conference was "Thank you all very much for coming out today"—rationalized that when he tapped his shoe on the shoe of an undercover cop in the adjoining stall at a public lavatory, it was not a case of "restroom leg syndrome," but rather his "wide stance," thereby breaking the feeble-excuse record made by Richard Nixon's secretary, Rose Mary Woods, during the Watergate scandal.

She had testified that, while transcribing one of his taped conversations, she answered a phone call, but when reaching for the Stop button on the recorder, she mistakenly hit the "Record" button next to it (unnecessarily), keeping her foot on the pedal, resulting in the infamous 18.5-minute gap. When asked to replicate that position, her extremely awkward posture caused pundits to question the validity of her explanation. She merely wanted to protect Nixon.

And Larry Craig merely wanted to remain a senator so that he could continue perpetuating anti-gay legislation. It all leads back to William Bennett—former education czar, drug czar, morality czar and gambling czar—when he was questioned about Gary Condit, the California congressman who led the effort to impeach Bill Clinton for lying about his affair with Monica Lewinsky. After Condit admitted that he himself had had an affair with an intern, Chandra Levy (not to mention the allegation that he was behind her disappearance and murder), a reporter asked Bennett whether he thought that Condit was being hypocritical.

"Hypocrisy," Bennett replied, "is better than having no values at all."

And hypocrisy is the ultimate target of this book. If I wrote it.

MORT SAHL'S BEST PUNCH LINE

On May 11, 2009, pioneer of political stand-up comedy Mort Sahl turned 82. In the early '50s, he broke through the tradition of jokes about airplane food, Asian drivers and frigid wives, and instead shared his wit and insights about such subject as militarism, racism and monogamy. I first met Sahl in 1953 when he was a guest speaker in a course I was taking at the New School for Social Research. I was inspired by his satirical approach to serious issues.

"Every word I do is improvised," he once told me. "I don't rehearse anything. I start it on stage."

At the beginning of his career, though, he would write key words on a rolled-up newspaper, which became his trademark prop. In 1960 he wrote jokes for presidential candidate John Kennedy, and Sahl's face, surrounded by balloons, was on the cover of *Time* magazine during the conventions in August. When Kennedy was killed in 1963, Sahl endangered his career and was blacklisted as a result of becoming an associate of New Orleans District Attorney Jim Garrison in his investigation of the JFK assassination.

In 1967 I was a guest on Sahl's TV show, which had been dealing outspokenly with contemporary controversies, so when his option wasn't renewed, ostensibly because of low ratings, there was much suspicion. But Sahl also had a nightly radio show and asked his listeners to write in to KTTV. By the time 31,000 letters arrived, the channel's executives had conveniently discovered another rating service and the option was renewed.

On the program, Sahl had a blackboard on which he wrote things in chalk like "We Demand Faith in the Future," and the audience applauded faithfully. He wanted to have a mock trial on the show as a preview of the Vietnam War

Crimes Tribunal, and he asked me to return and act as defense attorney. He wanted me to defend war criminals such as Lyndon Johnson, Dean Rusk and Robert McNamara. I agreed to do it. My plan was to plead insanity.

◆ ◆ ◆

On June 28, 2007, the Heartland Comedy Foundation, which sponsors fundraisers and assists comedians, honored Mort Sahl at the Wadsworth Theater in Brentwood. When my wife Nancy was 16, she listened over and over to his first album until she memorized it, just as she had done with the score of *My Fair Lady*. Now we were sitting two rows behind Sahl, watching him enjoy and appreciate one tribute after another by a gaggle of comedians.

There were the original gang members: Jonathan Winters (in character as an aging baseball star), Norm Crosby (master of malapropism) and Shelley Berman (doing his classic rotary-phone call, still dialing a number rather than pressing buttons).

And there was the newer breed: a surprise appearance by George Carlin (his set piece on contemporary schizophrenic man, followed by a film clip of his 1962 impression of Sahl), Jay Leno (charming, even with fat-joke material), Richard Lewis (skillfully balancing along the tightrope between dick comedy and Dick Cheney), Drew Carey (referring to the bus driver who told Rosa Parks to move to the back of the bus as "the father of the civil rights movement"), Harry Shearer introducing Kevin Nealon, and Bill Maher courting political incorrectness.

Woody Allen and Don Rickles sent their good wishes via video. The program announced, "Comedians scheduled to appear are subject to personal availability." Thus, David Steinberg and David Brenner were no-shows, and Larry King was replaced as host by Jack Riley, one of the patients in Bob Newhart's TV group-therapy ensemble.

Paula Poundstone, the only female comic there, resorted to her forte, asking an audience member, "What do you do for a living?" He was an attorney—giving her the opportunity to talk about her own problems with the law—and he turned out to have started the first Mort Sahl fan club in 1956. Poundstone asked if all the members of his fan club wore those cute cashmere pullover sweaters like Mort did.

Although all the performers topped off their regular schtick with praise for Sahl's comedic breakthrough, Albert Brooks was the most original and unique in the context of this occasion.

"I'm embarrassed tonight," he began. "And angry. And I'm confused. I don't know the people that produced this show at all. But I would strongly suggest that when they do an event like this again, they spend a little extra money and hire a real publicity firm to disseminate the information correctly. I was told that Mort Sahl passed away. So you can imagine my shock, my dismay and quite frankly my disappointment, when I arrived here this evening and saw him standing there.

"I worked very, very hard on this eulogy—and unlike other comedians tonight, I don't have a current act, I just can't pull ten minutes off the top of my head—so I do this, or I have nothing. I asked myself, 'What would the late Mort Sahl say?' I think he would have said, 'You do it.' Nobody appreciated a turn of a phrase, a beautifully written sentence, as much as he did. But then again I say, to the people that produced the show, 'If you don't wanna spring for full-blown publicity, please get someone who will talk to the talent.'"

And he started to read aloud: "Mort Sahl—1927 to 2007. Mort? We hardly knew you. I remember the last time I saw Mort alive. It was at a Starbucks near where I live. And now I wish I'd said the things that I really felt. I wish I'd said how much he influenced all of us here. How brave he was. I wish I'd have told him how much of an innovator he was. I wish I'd have told him how much I loved listening to his records. While he was here. But I didn't. All that I think I said that day was, 'Are you gonna finish that latte?'

"This should be a lesson to all of us. If you see someone that you love, don't ask for their food. Tell them how much they mean to you. Do you know what? On a night like this, I think we need to look on the positive side. From what was told to me, Mort didn't suffer. He died as he lived. In his sleep. It's at times like these that I think of what the great Alexander the Great said to his brother in the middle of a fierce fight. He said, 'I'm going home. I don't wanna fight anymore. You can take over. And try not to die.'

"If only I'd said that to Mort Sahl! That day in Starbucks. But I didn't. Actually I think, along with the latte comment, I also asked him if he were going to eat the scone. But you know what? I'm sure he knew what I meant. I'm sure he read into that freeloading comment the fact that I loved him. . . ."

Finally, Sahl himself took the stage—wearing, of course, his signature red pullover sweater.

"I've been very moved by everybody tonight," he said. "And I had a good time laughing. I want you to know it really did knock me out. And I also want you to know that I'll do it as long as they let me. I didn't want this to be a retirement party, you know. I'm still in business. And to reference that business—talking about the Bush administration—you know, I know the president, and he told me that he doesn't drink. He said, 'I don't need it, because I've been born again.' And what occurred to me in the moment was: If you had the rare opportunity to be born again, why would you come back as George Bush? . . . Cheney went to the hospital. Got an aneurysm in the right knee. You know, the one that replaced the left knee. Also, he's had four heart attacks and also a pacemaker. They're reconstructing Cheney, a Halliburton corporation. And they're overcharging him."

At one point, someone shouted, "Hey, Mort! You avoid 9/11 in your act. You always talked about the Warren Commission. You were all over it!"

"You hear that?" Sahl asked the audience, not realizing the critique came from a 9/11 Truth Movement member. "It was something to do with the Warren Commission. Well, you know that's how I went out of business for about twelve years. But I stuck to my guns, because I remember something [Bobby] Kennedy said: 'To all you with the guns out there. You may be able to slay the dreamer, but you haven't slain the dream.' I came to this because I really thought I was an American and really had the capacity to dream. You all know that if you watch *Turner Classic Movies*. That's what the movies were about—it was a dark place where people could fall in love and moral issues could be resolved. My grandfather came from Lithuania, although Lou Dobbs tried to stop him. . . . I dreamed that dream.

"When I started this act," he concluded, "although I was just lonesome and looking for a family, in a larger sense I saw it as a rescue mission for America . . . but I believe it more than ever, in spite of the odds. That the good guys'll win. . . . I tried to get to your funny bone and get into your head, but apparently I also got into your heart."

◆　◆　◆

In November 2007, I was supposed to open for Sahl at the Warner Grand Theater in San Pedro, California. The evening was a tribute to Jimmy Carter, who was in town building houses as part of his Habitat for Humanity campaign. The show began with a mini-musical, *Habitat*—featuring original lyrics for melodies from *Camelot*. Sahl had been there since 5:00 p.m., listening to the song rehearsals over and over, and his opening line would be "I hate *Camelot*." He had gotten so antsy while the singers were performing that he asked to be introduced immediately after them, and I would follow him.

So now I can honestly say that Mort Sahl once opened for me.

Currently, Sahl is a visiting professor at Claremont McKenna College, where he's been teaching courses such as "Critical Thinking" and "The Revolutionary's Handbook" (including his experience with Jim Garrison investigating the assassination of JFK) as well as a class in screenwriting. And he continues to perform regularly. At McCabes, for example, he observed that during the Republican debates, when the candidates were asked who didn't believe in evolution, a few raised their hands, and Sahl pointed out, "If you watched the debate, *you* wouldn't believe in evolution either." His targets have always included liberals and conservatives alike. As a news junkie, his material still has a sharp point of view, as opposed to easy-reference jokes about celebrities.

Recently, however, he adroitly poked fun at the public perception of a celebrity. A friend of mine was having his caffeine fix at a Starbucks in Los Angeles. He happened to be seated right near Sahl and recounts the following incident. A young woman who had just finished her coffee stopped to chat with Sahl. It was apparent that they knew each other. Then, as she started to leave, Robert Blake walked in. Sahl, loyal to his buddies, had been among those show-biz folks (including Quincy Jones, Sally Kirkland, Anthony Hopkins, Diane Sawyer and Barbara Walters) who visited Blake when he was in jail. Now, Sahl said to the young woman, "Do you know my good friend, Bob Blake?" Blake looked at her and said to Sahl, "She looks like a very nice person. She looks like she sleeps well at night."

Sahl paused, then said to Blake, "Well, she's got a clear conscience."

BARBARIAN AT THE GATE

When I first started doing stand-up comedy in the 1950s, I called myself Paul Maul and played the violin between jokes. Then I launched a satirical magazine, *The Realist*, in 1958, and stopped performing. But Lenny Bruce encouraged me to start again, only without that corny stage name and without using my violin as a crutch.

I began memorizing a long list of things that I could talk about on stage, and the order they were in. Lenny advised me to just go out on stage with a completely blank mind, but I wasn't ready for that yet.

In 1961, I opened at the Village Gate. Lenny couldn't come to my show because he was too busy getting arrested. Art D'Lugoff proved to be a most gracious host, taking care of details from placing an ad in the *Village Voice* to providing a sound engineer, namely Chip Monck, who would later become the disembodied voice at the Woodstock Festival. Most of all, D'Lugoff was supportive of my freedom to be irreverent and controversial. Here's an excerpt from that show:

"India has allocated $105 million dollars for birth control, but can you imagine the uproar there would be in this country? So don't tell me we're free from religious interference. I won't be satisfied until you can find an abortionist in the Yellow Pages. Until it's as socially acceptable as a nose job. Until people can start sending studio cards saying, 'Good luck on your abortion.' And don't say, 'Well that's different from birth control, that's murder.' Because, when you talk about abortion being murder and birth control not being murder, what's your focal point? The moment of conception. Before—*sí*. After—*no*. But this gets into all kinds of equivocal ramifications. Shouldn't a *douche* be ruled out? That's foul. It's a very tenuous thing. You're gonna have these rabble-rousers going around scrawling on signs in the subway: 'Zonite is a murderer!'"

D'Lugoff and I became friends. He was principled and generous. Like so many other performers, I developed a tremendous sense of loyalty to him. He always made me feel welcome at the Gate, and occasionally I would stop by to have a little chat. One afternoon, Ed Sanders—poet, peace activist and leader of the Fugs, a funky band that was the missing link between folk and punk—was there. We sat listening to an early rock group, the Byrds, rehearse for their performance that evening.

"Wow," I said, "they're pretty loud, huh?"

"You've gotta get *inside* the music," Ed explained.

The Gate continued to serve as a venue not only for an eclectic array of music, but also for benefits, forums and theatrical events.

It was purely a slip of Barbara Garson's tongue when, at an antiwar rally on the Berkeley campus in 1964, she referred to Lyndon Johnson's wife, Lady Bird, as "Lady MacBird." Then, in the wake of a demonstration to block the trains carrying troops that would end up fighting in Vietnam, she wrote a fifteen-minute takeoff on *MacBeth*, titled *MacBird*. She developed it into a full-length play, which she submitted to *The Realist*, but I rejected it because her targets had already been attacked so much in our pages.

However, when producers eventually began holding backers' auditions, I invested $3,000, since so many people who didn't read *The Realist* could now be exposed to this stage production. The play opened at the Gate. MacBird (LBJ) was played by Stacy Keach; Lady MacBird was played by Rue McClanahan; Robert Ken O'Dunc (Robert Kennedy) was played by William Devane.

The line that got the biggest reaction was when Robert Ken O'Dunc said, "I basically agree with both positions." In real life, Senator Kennedy had both come out against the bombing in Vietnam and voted for Johnson's supplementary budget to subsidize the war. *Voice* reporter and Robert Kennedy biographer Jack Newfield sent him a note: "To thine own self be true." I suggested that Kennedy would reply, "Out, damned spot."

◆ ◆ ◆

In 1965, Art D'Lugoff became upset when he read in the *New York Times* a quote by black poet LeRoi Jones, referring to slain white civil rights workers: "Those boys were just artifacts. They weren't real. If they went to Mississippi to assuage their leaking consciences, that's their business. I won't mourn for them. I have my own dead to mourn for." Jones then extended that lack of sympathy to the six million Jews who were slaughtered in Nazi Germany.

And so D'Lugoff invited LeRoi Jones to participate in a debate at the Gate, and he asked me to moderate the discussion. Jones agreed only because D'Lugoff promised him the free use of the Gate for a benefit for the Black Arts Repertory Theater. D'Lugoff and *Voice* columnist Nat Hentoff were also panelists. Jones was the star attraction, but he arrived an hour late.

"About the six million Jews," Hentoff said at one point, "you know, this is a tragedy within a tragedy, and I don't like it being used for rhetoric. The tragedy of those deaths—and there were many millions more Poles and Gypsies and Lord knows who, including Russians—is that nobody, including the Jews and the Poles and the Gypsies, what few of them are left, learned anything from it. I will agree that there is no real cohesive organization, but there are a number of Jewish organizations within the endemic tendency to disagree among Jews. But the fact is there was no outcry about the A-bomb in Hiroshima, there's no organized Jewish outcry about South Vietnam, there's no organized Jewish outcry about the whole skein of violence that is part of this country's foreign policy.

"Now the other part of this is—it seems to me so

simple, and yet it also indicates the lack of role-reversal ability—what the hell difference does it make to a guy in central Harlem or Bedford-Stuyvesant or the South Side of Chicago that six million Jews were killed? I mean you can't expect a guy on the Bowery—and this is true of a cracker as well, or a guy in Appalachia, or an Indian, or a Mexican—you can't expect him to be [theologian] Paul Tillich. He is hurting and he is hungry. And the only Jews he happens to see, probably, are the storekeepers who, for other economic and determinist reasons, are part of the ghetto. But you really can't bring in the six million Jews there, because it is not relevant."

D'LUGOFF: "I think you're dead wrong, Nat, and I think it's a disgrace—"

HENTOFF: "Are you going to take my mezuzah away?"

D'LUGOFF: "—because anybody who has the audacity to talk about any human beings that were killed or massacred or lynched the way you have . . . I think that you are saying something that, believe me, you may not like it, but I think it's anti-Semitic."

KRASSNER: "Not only is your mezuzah being taken *away*, but your foreskin is being given *back*."

Later, we got into a discussion about the white power structure.

JONES: "I do strongly believe that white America represents the most repressive force on the earth today."

D'LUGOFF: "Just what is it that you want *me* to do?"

JONES: "I want you to give this club to my father."

D'LUGOFF: "But I built this place with my own hands. Besides, this is a marginal operation."

JONES: "You're a drag."

D'LUGOFF: "Oh, yeah? You're a bigger drag."

The *New York Post* reported this as: "You're a bigot drag."

In 1971, five years after Lenny's death, Groucho Marx wrote to my publisher—"I predict that in time Paul Krassner will wind up as the only live Lenny Bruce"—and I took that note as my personal marching orders. I had moved to San Francisco, but the Gate was my stage away from home, and I would perform there every time I returned to New York. Here's an excerpt from a show I did at the Gate in 1981:

"There's definite sexism in the movie *E.T.* I mean, how do we know E.T. is a male? Because the little boy says, 'I'm keeping *him*.' This is a blatant male chauvinist assumption. I've seen *E.T.* and there's no penis. And even if there were, it would be human chauvinism to *assume* it was a penis. How do we know it's not just a spare battery holder for E.T.'s finger with the red light?"

Anyway, Art D'Lugoff never did give the Village Gate to Leroi Jones's father. And, although the building that once housed that venerable club may have changed, the spirit of the Gate remains a national treasure.

FEAR AND LAUGHING IN LAS VEGAS

"I'm covering this for *The Nation*," I told Jerry Seinfeld.

Chris Rock interjected, "The Nation of Islam?"

We were in Las Vegas (where Mayor Oscar Goodman had recently suggested that those who deface freeways with graffiti should have their thumbs cut off on TV) at the first annual Comedy Festival, a three-day laugh quest featuring some thirty-five shows. A ticket for all events cost $1,500.

There was a panel about comedy with Seinfeld, Rock,

Robert Klein and Garry Shandling, moderated by CNN news anchor Anderson Cooper. Shandling asked Cooper, "What do you do one night when you're just not feeling funny?" Seinfeld later received the first annual The Comedian award, given to a performer "who has most influenced and furthered the art of comedy." He said, "I'm honored, but awards are stupid. Every insurance company, hotel, car dealer—they get these jack-off trophies."

Seinfeld is best known for his observational humor, so after the presentation I asked if he'd ever done a political joke. He recalled one: "Anybody who wants to be president shows evidence of a brain that's not working too well."

The festival kickoff was a two-hour taping of a TV special, *Earth to America*, a comedic approach to raising consciousness about the environmental crisis. Executive producer Laurie David called it "a little bit of prime-time history." The show began with a film clip of her husband, Larry, star of *Curb Your Enthusiasm*, dressed as a modern Paul Revere, riding into Vegas on a horse and shouting, "Global warming is coming!"

"Coming to you from Las Vegas, the conscience of America," said emcee Tom Hanks.

RAY ROMANO: "I think it's very appropriate, we're trying to conserve energy in a town that uses more energy than any other town in the world."

BILL MAHER: "We have a president who thinks Kyoto is that guy his father threw up on in Japan."

WANDA SYKES: "I don't wanna go home and see my aunt out on the corner, trickin' for her medicine—'Tickle your balls for an anti-inflammatory?'"

At the after-party, two bodyguards were assigned to Laurie David; none to Robert F. Kennedy Jr. He had thanked the performers at *Earth to America* for volunteering their time. Actually, they got union scale. For the other shows, performers were highly paid.

The spirit of Lenny Bruce hovered over the festival. Robert Klein said Bruce was "good, funny, socially important—the best and highest a comedian could do." Perhaps Bruce's most audacious onstage moment was in 1962 when he became the voice of Holocaust orchestrator Adolf Eichmann, in a German accent: "My defense—I was a soldier. I saw the end of a conscientious day's effort. I watched through the portholes. I saw every Jew burned and turned into soap. Do you people think yourselves better because you burned your enemies at long distance with missiles without ever seeing what you had done to them? Hiroshima *auf Wiedersehen*. . . ."

Bruce was arrested for obscenity that night.

That controversial portrayal of Eichmann had particularly inspired Bill Maher, who lost his ABC show, *Politically Incorrect* , because six days after 9/11 he said, "We have been the cowards, lobbing cruise missiles from 2,000 miles away—*that's* cowardly. Staying in the airplane when it hits the building, say what you want about it, it's not cowardly." Of course, the hijackers couldn't have gotten out of the plane at that point even if they wanted to.

After the terrorist attacks, Larry King asked Maher how soon it would be all right to be funny again. "So like two months, that's a good time? One month is a good time?" King also asked Dr. Andrew Weil, "Are bulimics throwing up more often?"

Less than three weeks after 9/11, at a roast for Hugh Hefner, Gilbert Gottfried began, "Tonight I'm going to perform under my Muslim name, Hasn't bin Laid." He got a big laugh, but when he closed with, "I have to catch a flight to Los Angeles—I can't get a direct flight—they said they have to stop at the Empire State Building first," the audience booed.

Which brings us to Homeland Security. I had gone through a metal detector at the airport, and again, along with 4,145 others, at The Colosseum in Caesars Palace. I had to take my shoes off before I could fly, and now I got wanded to preserve the safety of comedians. My weapon, a tape recorder, was temporarily confiscated. There was even a sign warning "Heckling Will Not Be Tolerated." Would-be hecklers were informed that they'd be removed from the concert hall if they heckled a performer and would not be given refunds.

Jon Stewart was in top form: "That suicide-bomb married couple were gonna blow themselves up at a wedding in Jordan. I'd say—relationship issues." "The Emergency Broadcast System is a test of your remote control." "Posting the Ten Commandments is as effective as posting 'Employees Must Wash Hands.'" "Senator Bill Frist, he's a doctor and he says that AIDS could be transmitted from sweat and tears. Not unless your penis weeps while you're fucking somebody."

Although Stewart was used to the TV audiences who virtually all agreed with his stance on Iraq, here, when he talked about George Bush's renewed push to justify the war, he couldn't help but notice that those in the front rows were not laughing and applauding like those "in the less expensive seats. *You* like the way things are going just fine." He began pointing at different sections of the orchestra: "*You* run Halliburton. . . . *You* make bombs. . . . *You* own NASCAR."

Lewis Black, seen periodically on *The Daily Show*, is an incisive and outspoken stand-up comic, but when he performed at the annual Radio and Television Correspondents Dinner, he found himself sitting next to Dick Cheney, one of his favorite targets. I asked Black how that went.

"It worked out fine," he told me, "as I had destroyed my usual act, in the name of entertainment. As long as you take the gig, you should be good at it, and I feel that nothing would have been accomplished if I had pissed all over them. I didn't want to spend the next week talking to reporters about it. I stopped and talked to the vice president as I left the dais. One of his closest friends is the brother of a close friend of mine who passed away a number of years ago. I asked him to please say 'Hi' to his friend for me. I hadn't seen him in quite some time. So basically I asked the vice president to be my messenger boy, and hopefully it would keep him out of trouble for a few minutes."

There had been a rumor that Dave Chappelle would do a three-hour set, but he did just one hour. "You can't do three hours in Las Vegas," Chris Rock remarked. "They want people to get out to the casinos and gamble." Chappelle's appearance at the festival was the first event to be sold out. After all, he had fled to South Africa, leaving behind his successful *Chappelle's Show* and a $50 million development deal. Now there were six security guards in red jackets sitting on the floor at the foot of the stage, facing the audience.

"Holy shit," were Chappelle's first words in response to the ovation when he walked on stage. "Bottom line: If you haven't heard about me, I'm fucking insane!" And later: "Kanye did the bravest thing." (After Hurricane Katrina, rapper Kanye West said, "George Bush doesn't care about black people.") "The bravest. I'm gonna miss him. I'm not gonna risk my career to tell white people obvious things. I saw what happened to the Dixie Chicks." Still later: "We have to work on our vocabulary. 'Minorities': a high-class way of calling you a nigger to your face. 'Get away from my car, you minority!'" "Vicente Fox said that Mexican immigrants do jobs that not even blacks do. He is right. Till I see a nigger selling oranges on the street, I can't talk." "I'm not a crackhead. I was only living out my dream: to get to the top of show business and go back to Africa."

Unlike Richard Pryor's confessional comedy, Chappelle did not say what precipitated his departure to fulfill his "dream." Pryor had the ability to reach into his unconscious and turn himself inside out for the benefit of an audience. Like a comedic alchemist transforming pain into laughter, he revealed on stage the anguished private dialogues he'd held—with his heart during an attack, and with the pipe through which he had freebased cocaine—balancing on the cusp of tragedy and absurdity.

Pryor was self-educated, and on his television show he advised children to turn off their TV sets and read books. On the day Pryor died in December 2005, Dick Gregory and Mort Sahl performed at McCabe's in Los Angeles. Gregory eulogized Pryor as "a true genius," and Sahl reminisced about Gene McCarthy, who had died that same day.

After the invasion of Iraq, the late-night talk-show monologues—by Jay Leno, David Letterman, Conan O'Brien—helped demonize Saddam Hussein and these hosts served as cheerleaders for the war. But as the unbrainwashing of America goes, so goes the late-night talk-show monologue. O'Brien, for example: "Congress stepped up the pressure on President Bush to come up with an exit strategy for Iraq. Today, Bush said, 'I have an exit strategy—I'm leaving office in 2008.'" And sleazy government officials are now easy-listening joke references. Triumph the Insult Comic Dog: "What does Karl Rove have for breakfast? . . . Bagel with a smear."

What's shocking about Lenny Bruce these days is the fact that he was punished for his political and religious views in the guise of violating obscenity laws. What's obscene by current standards is that his comment after channeling Adolf Eichmann would end up in a police report as follows: "Then talking about the war he stated, 'If we would have lost the war, they would have strung [President Harry] Truman up by the balls.'"

Lenny was a lone voice back then, but irreverence has since become an industry.

DON IMUS MEETS MICHAEL RICHARDS

In the early 1960s, Dick Gregory called his autobiography *Nigger*, because, he explained, "I told my mama if she hears anybody shout 'nigger,' they're just advertising my book." Richard Pryor called one of his albums *That Crazy Nigger*, and wrote an article for *The Realist* about the disproportionate number of blacks fighting and dying in Vietnam, titled "Uncle Sam Wants You Dead, Nigger!" After a visit to Africa, he reclaimed his heritage, promising not to use that word again. And then there was Lenny Bruce, on stage one night, riding an invisible unicycle as he balanced his way along a tightrope into uncharted comedic territory:

"The reason I don't get hung up with, well, say,

integration, is that by the time Bob Newhart is integrated, I'm bigoted. And anyway, Martin Luther King, Bayard Rustin are geniuses, the battle's won. By the way, are there any niggers here tonight? [*In outraged whisper, as if an audience member*] 'What did he say? Are there any *niggers* here tonight? Jesus Christ! Is that cruel. Does he have to get that low for laughs? Wow! Have I ever talked about the *schwarzes* when the *schwarzes* had gone home? Or spoken about the Moulonjohns when they'd left? Or placated some Southerner by absence of voice when he ranted and raved about *nigger nigger nigger*?'

"[*In his own voice*]: Are there any niggers here tonight? I know that one nigger who works here, I see him back there. Oh, there's two niggers, customers, and, ah, *aha!* Between those two niggers sits one kike—man, thank God for the kike! Uh, two kikes. That's two kikes, and three niggers, and one spic. One spic—two, three spics. One mick. One mick, one spic, one hick, thick, funky, spunky boogey. And there's another kike. Three kikes. Three kikes, one guinea, one greaseball. Three greaseballs, two guineas. Two guineas, one hunky funky lace-curtain Irish mick. That mick spic hunky funky boogey. Two guineas plus three greaseballs and four boogeys makes usually three spics. Minus two Yid spic Polack funky spunky Polacks. [*Auctioneer's voice*] 'Five more niggers! Five more niggers!' [*Gambler's voice*] 'I pass with six niggers and eight micks and four spics.'

"[*In his own voice*] The point? That the word's suppression gives it the power, the violence, the viciousness. If President Kennedy got on television and said, 'Tonight I'd like to introduce the niggers in my cabinet,' and he yelled 'nigger-nigger-nigger-nigger-nigger-nigger-nigger' at every nigger he saw, 'boogey-boogey-boogey-boogey-

boogey-nigger-nigger-nigger-nigger' till nigger didn't mean anything any more, till nigger lost its meaning, you'd never make any four-year-old nigger cry when he came home from school. Screw 'Negro!' Oh, it's so good to say 'Nigger!' Boy! 'Hello, Mr. Nigger, how're you?'"

Four decades later, Dave Chappelle on his TV show played a man delivering milk to the all-white family, the Niggars, and he did indeed say, "Hello, Mr. Niggar, how're you?" But consider the contrast between Lenny's good-natured, poetic routine and Michael Richards' mean-spirited, uncontrollable outburst. In November 2006, at the Laugh Factory in Los Angeles, in response to heckling from a table of four African Americans (three men and a woman), he suddenly became enraged with repressed hatred:

"Shut up! Fifty years ago we'd hang you upside down with a fucking fork up your ass! [*Laughter in the audience, apparently unaware of the heckler's race and that the reference is to lynching*] You can talk, you can talk, you can talk, now you're brave, motherfucker! Throw his ass out! He's a nigger! He's a nigger! He's a nigger!"

A WOMAN IN THE AUDIENCE: "Oh my God!"

"A nigger! Look, there's a nigger! [*Imitating reactions in the audience*] 'Oooh! Oooh!' All right, you see, this shocks you, it shocks you to see what lies beneath your stupid motherfuckers!"

A MAN AT THE HECKLER TABLE: "That wasn't called for."

"What was uncalled-for? It's uncalled-for for you to interrupt my ass, you cheap motherfucker! You guys have been talking and talking and talking."

VOICE FROM THE AUDIENCE: "Calm down."

"What's the matter with you? Is this too much for you to handle?"

"I said calm down."

"They're gonna arrest me for calling a black man a nigger? Wait a minute, where's he going?"

"That was uncalled-for, you fucking cracker-ass motherfucker!"

"You calling me cracker-ass, nigger?

"Fucking white boy!"

"Are you threatening me?"

"We'll see what's up."

"Oh, it's a big threat. That's how you get back at the man."

"You're just not funny. That's why you're a reject. Never had no shows, never had no movies. *Seinfeld*, that's it."

"Oh, I guess you got me there. You're absolutely right. I'm just a wash-up. Gotta stand on this stage."

"That's it, we've had it. Niggers—that's un-fucking-called-for. That ain't necessary."

"Well, you interrupted me, pal. That's what you get when you interrupt the white man, don't you know."

"Uncalled-for, that was uncalled-for."

"You see, there's still those words, those words, those words."

Richards then walked off stage. In the days that followed, seemingly stunned at his own racist rage, he apologized on the media again and again as best he could. Meanwhile, the n-word was banned at the Laugh Factory. On a Sunday night there, at the weekly "Chocolate Sundaes" showcase of mostly African American performers, Damon Wayans announced, "Welcome to Nigger Night." He proceeded to say "nigger" fifteen more times in a twenty-minute routine, and was fined $20 for each one, plus he was banned from performing there for three months. Contrariwise, the Comedy Union club in Hollywood actually encouraged comics to say "nigger" at least once during their set on a particular night.

Paul Mooney used to say, "Well, white folks, you shouldn't have ever made up the word. I say nigger 100 times every morning. It makes my teeth white." But now he vowed never to resort to that word again. "I've used it and abused it," he explained, "and I never thought I'd say this, but Michael Richards is Dr. Phil—he cured me." On the HBO show *Real Time*, Chris Rock responded to Bill Maher's mention of Richards' use of "the n-word" with mock innocence: "He said nigger? Nicotine?"

Jamie Foxx defended the use of "nigger," but only by black people. On the night before Martin Luther King Day in 2007, he began his monologue at the Borgata in Atlantic City: "I'm an Oscar winner, but I'm a nigger too." Referring to the Richards incident, Foxx said, "He was just calling us niggers like it was the '50s. Nigger, nigger, with a 'e-r.' Then they said we can't use the word 'nigger' any more. That's my shit. I need it. I need the word to describe certain things, because at a certain level of excitement, I need to tell you how the shit was, and there ain't no other word that helps me say that better than that word. White people, you can't use it."

However, at the Improv, white comic Andy Dick was in the audience, busy heckling fellow performer Ian Bagg, when he got out of his seat, jumped onstage and began joking with Bagg. The subject of Michael Richards came up, but they quickly moved past it. As Dick exited the stage, though, he suddenly grabbed the microphone and shouted at the audience, "You're all a bunch of niggers!" The club issued this statement: "The Improv is aware of Andy Dick's behavior on Saturday night. Our policy is that material deemed offensive by both famous and up-and-coming comedians is judged on a case-by-case basis. In this particular case, Mr. Dick was commenting on a current event. Was it intelligent? No. Was it funny? No. But was it racist? No. It was not directed at any audience member in particular and although it was in bad taste, it was a comment on the Michael Richards fiasco."

Patti Smith's song "Rock N Roll Nigger" was later covered by Marilyn Manson. Rapper Nas decided to title his album *Nigger*. On *Mad TV*, a sketch about black actors dressed like pimps waiting to audition for a part turned out to be a commercial for a candy bar called "Sniggers." And in an episode of *Curb Your Enthusiasm* titled "The N-Word," Larry David was in a bathroom stall when he happened to overhear somebody on a cell phone refer to a "300-pound nigger." David was shocked, and later, on a couple of occasions when he was describing that incident—and quoting the offending phrase—a different black person happened to overhear him each time and became furious.

The NAACP Philadelphia Youth Council held a mock funeral for the n-word. And, at the NAACP annual convention in Detroit, a horse-drawn carriage pulled a pine casket with a black wreath on top, signifying the death of the n-word. In February 2007, a historically black school in Alabama held a four-day event titled the 'N' Surrection Conference at Stillman College. Its goal was to challenge the use of the n-word "through the use of intelligent dialogue and a thorough examination of black history." Kovan Flowers, co-founder of AbolishTheNWord.com, said that striking the word "nigger" from use would help set an example for other races. "We can't say anything to Hispanics, or whites or whoever unless we stop using it ourselves," he said. "It's the root of the mindset that's affecting why people are low, from housing to jobs to education."

Community activist Tim Robinson pointed out that blacks don't have a problem using the word "nigga" because it's distinctly different and is considered a term of endearment when they say it to each other. He said, "It was 'nigger' which was the bad word, but you've got our people that just went and changed it up a bit." The late rapper Tupac Shakur was credited with legitimizing "nigga" with his song "N.I.G.G.A." which stood for "Never Ignorant Getting Goals Accomplished." In an interview in the June 2008 issue of *Blender* magazine, rapper Lil Wayne used the word "nigga" twelve times.

The first season of Aaron McGruder's TV adaptation of his controversial comic strip *The Boondocks* on the Cartoon Network angered Al Sharpton and other black activists by the show's frequent use of "nigger." The second season was scheduled to devote an entire episode to "The N-Word." Co-executive producer Rodney Barnes explained, "You can't bury 'nigger.' It's like a vampire. It's going to live forever. And we can't let the fans down. Why be responsible now?" On the other hand, on the short-lived series *Cavemen*, the cavemen referred to themselves as "maggers," but this was considered racist, and the word "magger" quickly disappeared from the sitcom's scripts.

Attorney Gloria Allred tried to arrange an informal three-member "jury" of a retired judge and two lawyers to decide "whether they think, under the facts and the law, Michael Richards should be accountable and, if so, in what way. We want accountability, and we want the public to understand the significance of the n-word and how it has hurt" her clients. Richards' lawyer, Douglas Mirell, said that while Richards' comments were "inappropriate, they are not legally actionable" and that if Richards faced mediation or a lawsuit, he intended to oppose a cash settlement under his constitutional right to free speech—an incorrect claim, since the First Amendment applies only to censorship by the government.

("Actually," free-speech attorney David Blasband informs me, "the First Amendment does not provide an absolute defense where a public official or public figure sues for defamation. They can still prevail if they can show that the defendant knew or should have known that the publication was false. This is called Constitutional malice, but is a formidable burden for the plaintiff.")

Elayne Boosler came to Richards' defense in a blog on *Huffington Post*:

"Words won't kill you unless they are 'Ready, aim, fire!' Now that some time has gone by since the Michael Richards rant, let's talk about the true victim of the 'n-word'—stand-up comedy. The *Los Angeles Times* continues to feature articles on the Laugh Factory, focusing on further 'n-word' developments, and on black comedians lamenting the loss of their use of the 'n-word' at the club. They're determined to say it, even though the club owner is fining them for it.

"When I watch the majority of black comedians on cable and in clubs, I am amazed the TV version of *Amos and Andy* was called racist, and canceled due to the main characters speaking less than perfect English in their rhythms. (We're not discussing the radio show, which was done in blackface before television and which, by the way, was voted into the Radio Hall of Fame last week.) Those men had jobs, wore suits, had beautiful wives in earrings and pearls, and ate at tables with tablecloths. They were a classy version of *The Honeymooners*, the ostensible white welfare show.

"By comparison, the 'comedians' on cable seem to be making Klan recruitment films. There is such a dearth of dignity, but most of all, such a lack of comedy, that every time I try to watch I say out loud to the performer on TV, 'Hey, I've got the Kingfish on the phone here, he'd like an apology.' These shows have reinvented comedy as style over substance, rhythm over writing. I can't discern a joke, let alone root for the person up there. Between the 'n-word,' the 'mf-word,' and 'bitches' and 'hos' (talk about insulting half the population every waking hour of the day), they have annihilated stand-up comedy. Those words have made it possible for people to fill an hour set without five actual minutes of comedy. Maybe stand-up comedy could hire Gloria Allred to sue on its behalf, for a proper sum for not only hurting its feelings, but destroying its legacy. (Allred, what a great feminist. 'We're going to find a retired judge and let him decide.')

"The rule about heckling is this: You fire at a cop, get ready to die. Yelling 'You're not funny' at a comic is firing with an AK. Hurt your feelings? Tough. Anything goes for hecklers, including excessive force. I lay myself bare up here, at my most vulnerable, you shoot me in the chest, I will kill you if I can. You know why Richards looked so shell-shocked at his own outburst? Because he's not a racist, he was simply in the zone. Comedy clubs are like Indian reservations. They are their own country. I don't think he should have apologized. You pay your money and you take your chances, step right up.

"Jesse Jackson and Al Sharpton, far from demanding apologies, should have apologized to Bill Cosby, who tried to point out the heartbreak and social defeat of how some blacks are undercutting their own dignity and chances (did you see *Queens of Comedy*?). It's one thing to use the 'n-word' when you are an original, like Chris Rock or Bernie Mac, or if you're a genius, like Richard Pryor. It's another matter when you don't have the talent to co-opt the enemy. These currently enraged black leaders are about ten years too late in their outrage, and they are mad at the wrong person. By the way, the best black comedian I ever saw was Marsha Warfield. She cut to the bone of race relations, was brilliantly funny, as well as intense, challenging, and seething with rage, and she never used the 'n-word' once. . . .

"When I started doing stand-up in 1973, the women working in comedy were the caricatures of their time; housewives who hated sex, loved jewelry, hated their husbands, hated themselves, etc. My oath to myself was that I would do nothing, no humor, no matter how easy it would have been, that propagated any of those images of women. I had to work harder, write better, face resistance, lose opportunity, to present a funny woman who was a worthwhile human being deserving of respect and dignity, and who could entertain not just a niche audience, but people. I don't see too many comics striving for that on cable. You can't legislate the end of the 'n-word.' Nobody can ever tell a comic not to say something, it runs against a comic's soul. Don't take the 'n-word' out of your act because someone wants to ban it. Take it out because you are replacing it with actual comedy."

Editorial cartoonist Mr. Fish depicted Jesse Jackson saying, "In light of the Michael Richards tirade, I'm calling for the immediate removal of the letter 'N' from the alphabet so that racism will no longer exist in this country." I decided to send a contribution to the NAACP in support of their anti-discrimination efforts, and I made the check out to the AACP.

◆ ◆ ◆

On *60 Minutes* in 1998, Don Imus told Mike Wallace that his show had someone specifically assigned to do "nigger jokes." In 2000, *Newsday*'s Philip Noble monitored the Imus show for months, then cited numerous examples of his racist, homophobic and misogynist references. In 2001, Imus promised syndicated columnist Clarence Page that he wouldn't make racist comments about black athletes any more.

But in April 2007, on the morning after the mostly black Rutgers University women's basketball team had reached the finals of the NCAA women's basketball championship, Imus offhandedly remarked, "That's some nappy-headed hos." Calls for his removal from the airwaves were made by public figures ranging from then-Senator Barack (not black enough) Obama to Al (too black) Sharpton, from feminist Eleanor (not woman enough) Smeal to Jesse ("Let's go to Hymietown") Jackson. Although Imus proceeded to apologize all over the media, ranging from Sharpton's radio program to the *Today* show, he felt that he was only following the lyrics of black rappers, from the Wu Tang Clan ("nappy-headed niggaz") to Ludacris (boasting of random "hos in different area codes").

Platinum-seller Chamillionaire admitted, "I've always used the n-word," but after he went on tour and saw mostly whites in the audience lip-synching it along with him, he announced that his new album, *Ultimate Victory*, would not include the n-word, explaining, "I'm not going to say the the n-word on this one because when I go back on the road and I start performing, I don't want them to be saying it, like me teaching them." He said this conversion was a moral issue and not a result of the backlash against Imus. Snoop Dogg said that rappers "are not talking about no collegiate basketball girls who have made it to the next level in education and sports. We're talking about hos that's in the 'hood that ain't doing shit that's trying to get a nigger for his money."

In 1992, hip-hop mogul Russell Simmons had stated that "oppression of artistic expression, like any sort of oppression, should not be tolerated." In 2007, he told reporters that offensive references in hip-hop "may be uncomfortable for some to hear" but that his job wasn't to censor expression. Yet, only one week later, in the wake of Imusgate, he joined Al Sharpton's insistence that broadcasters should ban "bitch," "ho" and "nigger." Sharpton, who had announced to the press in 1995 that record-label executives shouldn't "cave in" to right-wingers wanting to censor lyrics because it would "infringe on our First Amendment rights," now justified his turnaround because James Brown on his deathbed had urged him to "be more aggressive in cleaning up the music."

In November 2007, the Los Angeles City Council unanimously approved a resolution banning the n-word. Other cities had already passed similar measures. Two months before the Imus incident, on the first day of Black History Month, New York City Councilman Leroy Comrie successfully sponsored a "symbolic moratorium on the use of the n-word." Ironically, at a hearing on Comrie's resolution, the word "nigger" was said nearly fifty times in less than two hours. The founder of the Ban the N-Word Movement, Marcia Harris, alone, said "nigger" nineteen times. (One man who didn't say it was Atlanta-based attorney Roy Miller, who managed to get the word stricken from the Funk & Wagnalls dictionary.)

A few days later, inside Harlem's Uptown Jeans clothing store, the voice of rapper 50 Cent, one of whose songs is titled "To All My Niggers," blared over the loudspeaker, "Nigger you front you gon' get it, okay, now maybe I said it."

"What difference does it make if they ban the n-word?" a bookseller asked. "Ban police brutality. Ban racial profiling. Ban that. Forget the n-word." Four months after the plethora of rap-lyrics criticism that followed the Imus incident, New York City Councilwoman Darlene Mealy tried unsuccessfully to ban the words "ho" and "bitch" (which was referred to in the attempted legislation as the "b-word.)" Basketball star Isiah Thomas said that although it's wrong for a black man to call a black woman a bitch, it's much worse for a white man to do it.

On April 9, 2007, CBS Radio announced it was suspending the *Imus in the Morning* show for two weeks. Two days later, a Pennsylvania radio station fired a disc jockey for urging listeners to mimic the Imus epithet. That same day, MSNBC decided to cancel its simulcast of Imus's radio show. Although sponsors—General Motors, GlaxoSmithKline, Procter & Gamble, American Express, Sprint Nextel, Bigelow Tea, Staples—had pulled their commercials from the Imus show, NBC denied that the loss of advertising motivated his cancellation. The next day, CBS fired Imus. Sponsors had already dropped out, and others were threatening to do so.

Imus hired attorney Martin Garbus, who annnounced that Imus would sue CBS for $120 million, since they had contractually encouraged Imus. A clause acknowledged that his program was "unique, extraordinary, irreverent, intellectual, topical, controversial." Garbus said the firing was "unconstitutional," which could be considered an accurate claim, since the FCC is a government agency. Imus and CBS settled out of court. Meanwhile, a clue in the *New York Times* crossword puzzle was "Fired celeb," and the correct answer was "Imus."

In a *Los Angeles Times* op-ed, civil rights attorney Constance Rice, sounding somewhat like Lenny Bruce, wrote, "But rest assured, the Imus crew has plenty of kike, wetback, mick, spick, dago, Jap, Chink, redneck and unprintable Catholic priest jokes too. Not to mention the rabid homophobia and occasional Islamophobia. . . . Imus' remarks were racist, offensive and, given that these athletes are not fair targets, out of bounds. There is no excuse for what he said. But there's also no basis for firing him or ending his show. Firing Imus for racist riffs would be like firing Liberace for flamboyance. It's what he does. More to the point, Imus should only be fired when the black artists who make millions of dollars rapping about black bitches and hos lose *their* recording contracts. Black leaders should denounce Imus and boycott him and call for his head only after they do the same for the misogynist artists with whom they have shared stages, magazine covers and the awards shows."

Washington Post media critic Howard Kurtz—whom Imus had once referred to as "a boner-nosed, beanie-wearing Jewboy"—stated, "I do not believe Imus is a bigot—not a man who raised millions for cancer-stricken kids of all races to stay at his New Mexico ranch." *New York Times* columnist Frank Rich argued in favor of free speech, and that Bill O'Reilly should be allowed to say "wetbacks," a term used as dismissive shorthand for undocumented Mexicans. O'Reilly claimed that he was actually searching for the word "coyote."

Gloria Allred represented a member of the Rutgers team who planned to sue Imus and CBS for slander and defamation of character, charging that his comment had damaged her reputation. This was reminiscent of the joke about a public speaker who states, "The trouble with women is that they take things too personally"—then a woman in the audience stands up and says, "I do not." In September 2007, the basketball player's frivolous lawsuit was withdrawn, ostensibly so she could focus on her education.

In April 2007, CBS fired the hosts of *The Dog House with JV and Elvis* after they placed an on-air order to a Chinese restaurant for "slimp flied lice" and compared food items to body parts. "In the wake of the Imus case," said New York City Councilman John Liu, "it would have been maddening to the communty if these idiots did not get fired."

The next month, XM Satellite Radio suspended shock jocks Opie and Anthony for thirty days after they aired a segment with "Homeless Charlie." When they mentioned Laura Bush, Condoleezza Rice and Queen Elizabeth, he said about each, "I'd love to fuck that bitch." Although the station is not subject to FCC regulation or punishment, it did need FCC approval to merge with satellite-radio competitor Sirius. In 2002, the pair had been fired by CBS Radio for broadcasting a call from two listeners who said they were having sex in St. Patrick's Cathedral. Now they expressed sympathy for Don Imus, saying that his career was "gone, just because he was trying to entertain people." In fact, though, Imus would be returning to radio, on ABC.

Meanwhile, Glenn Beck called antiwar activist Cindy Sheehan "a pretty big prostitute," then softened that epithet to "tragedy pimp." Michael Savage called Barbara Walters "a mental prostitute" and "a double-talking slut." *GQ* editor Jim Nelson, parodying *The Secret*, advised readers to "visualize what you want (an Alfa Romeo? Leather pants? An Asian whore?), think positively and the universe will make it happen to you," arousing the ire of the Asian American Journalists Association and the Asian American Justice Association.

Nobel Prize winner James Watson told the *London Times* that he was "inherently gloomy about the prospect of Africa" because "all our social policies are based on the fact that their intelligence is the same as ours, whereas all the testing says not really." Bill O'Reilly was more succinct when he expressed his surprise about eating at a restaurant in Harlem because black patrons weren't yelling at the waitress, "Hey, where's my motherfucking iced tea?"

Presidential candidates John McCain and Mitt Romney used the racially offensive term "tar baby" and later both apologized. On her Comedy Central series, Sarah Silverman insisted to an African American waiter that the Holocaust was worse than slavery, then as a social experiment she did the rest of the show in minstrel-blackface. In *Tropic Thunder*, Robert Downey Jr. played a method actor who tints his skin black for the role of an African American soldier. Black comic Sheryl Underwood called Monica

Lewinsky "an amateur ho." And Don Imus referred to his wife Deirdre, an environmental activist, as "the green ho."

In July 2008, a live microphone caught Jesse Jackson whispering that he wanted to cut Barack Obama's nuts off for "telling niggers how to behave." Whereupon Jamie Masada—owner of the Laugh Factory, who had originally joined Jackson's call for a ban on the n-word after Michael Richards' outburst—wanted to fine Jackson just as he does whenever a comedian says "nigger" on his stage, the fine being donated to the Museum of Tolerance, only it's been raised from $20 to $50. Inflation everywhere.

And finally, the Black Panther Party's mission statement, in a masterstroke of co-option, is now featured as the slogan in a commercial for the Oral-B battery-operated toothbrush: "Power to the People."

THE GREAT MUHAMMAD CARTOON CONTROVERSY

As a secular humanist, I find it simultaneously tragic and absurd to witness so much unspeakable anguish caused by religious wars in the Middle East being fought over deities in whose existence I disbelieve—Jehovah vs. Allah, Jesus vs. Muhammad—and, as a free speech advocate, to witness the death and destruction triggered by Danish cartoonists' depictions of the latter prophet. There are basic principles of semantics concerning symbolism—the menu is not the meal; the map is not the territory—which serve only to intensify both the tragedy and the absurdity.

"Okay," said Pulitzer Prize–winning editoral cartoonist Joel Pett, "let's put down our pens and swords, and recap. Danish editors, concerned about self-censorship over Islamic imagery, challenged cartoonists to portray

Muhammad, an Islamic no-no. Outraged Muslim clerics pressured the Danes to apologize, outraging more European editors, who reprinted the cartoons, outraging many more Muslims. The clerics circulated them, leading to riots throughout the Muslim world.

"Meanwhile, fearing editorial censors, not to mention firebrand jihadists, U.S. cartoonists did a lot of self-censoring. Plenty of people pointed to what they said was the hypocrisy of the Muslim reaction to the Danish cartoons, given how often the Arab press publishes hateful images of Jews. An Iranian editor raised the stakes when he announced that his paper would challenge cartoonists to debunk the Holocaust, a crime in several European countries."

One such cartoon had Holocaust victim Anne Frank in bed with Adolf Hitler after having sex. Hitler says, "Write *this* one in your diary, Anne." Beyond that, the British revisionist historian David Irving decided that he would plead guilty to charges of Holocaust denial when he appeared in a Vienna court. He had been held in an Austrian prison for several months. He said that he did not consider himself to be a Holocaust denier but that he had no choice but to plead guilty as charged. "Under the law I've got no alternative," he stated—but, he added, "I deny that I'm a Holocaust denier," as though he had been inspired by Groucho Marx, who once declared, "I deny everything, because I lie about everything. And everything I *deny* is a lie."

"In the end," concluded cartoonist Pett, "the fine line between respectful deference and timid self-censorship is only clearly defined by sticking your toe, or your neck, out over it. Outraged reaction is a daily byproduct of strong satire, but let's be clear: Cartoons don't burn embassies, people do."

An offending cartoon reprinted in Geneva's *Le Temps* and Budapest's *Magyar Hirlap* showed an imam telling suicide bombers to stop because Heaven had run out of virgins to reward them. In September 2007, after Swedish cartoonist Lars Vilks drew a picture of a dog with Muhammad's head on it, the Islamic State of Iraq placed a bounty of $100,000 on the head of Vilks—"$150,000 if he is slaughtered like a lamb"—and a $50,000 reward for killing the editor of the newspaper that published the cartoon. Vilks responded, "I suppose this makes my art project a bit more serious. It's also good to know how much one is worth." Police took him to a secret location and told him that he could not return home because of the death threat.

However, the German newspaper *Die Welt*, which reprinted the Danish cartoons, editorialized: "We'd take Muslim protests more seriously if they weren't so hypocritical. The imams were quiet when Syrian television showed Jewish rabbis as cannibals in a prime-time series"—much like the late Isaac Hayes's delayed departure from *South Park* because animated kids had poked fun at *his* "religion," Scientology, though he had never complained about their use of Christianity as a satirical target. Although *South Park* allowed a scene in which Jesus Christ and George Bush fling excrement at each other, Comedy Central censors yanked their depiction of Muhammad, prompting critics to suggest that the network be renamed Cowardly Central.

A military commander for the resurgent Taliban in Afghanistan was quoted in Arab newspapers as claiming that the Taliban had recruited at least 100 new suicide bombers as a result of the cartoons. And the BBC reported that the Arab boycott of Danish food products was costing the Danish company Aria millions per day. The company complained that full-page ads they took out in Saudi Arabia, explaining that they had nothing to do with the cartoons, had no effect. In Iran, as if imitating our own country changing the name of French fries to "Freedom fries," those wishing to purchase Danish pastry now have to ask for "Roses of the Prophet Muhammad."

In November 2007, Sudan charged a British teacher, Gillian Gibbons, with inciting religious hatred—a crime punishable by forty lashes, six months in prison and a fine—because she had allowed her 7-year-old students to name a teddy bear Muhammad. She was arrested after some parents of her students objected. Although Muhammad is a common name among Muslims, they considered it an affront to use his name for a toy. After worldwide indignation against the Sudanese government, followed by a quickie seven-hour trial, she was found guilty of "insulting the faith of Muslims" and sentenced to fifteen days in prison.

In the United States, *Harper's* magazine published reprints of the original Danish Muhammad cartoons, along with an article by Art Spiegelman relating the history of the controversy, providing his explanation and review of the cartoons and giving each one a rating, from one to four bombs.

Among those U.S. newspapers that declined to reprint the Danish cartoons, only the *Boston Phoenix* editors admitted that they made the decision "out of fear of retaliation from the international brotherhood of radical and bloodthirsty Islamists who seek to impose their will on those who do not believe as they do. This is, frankly, our primary reason for not publishing any of the images in question. Simply stated, we are being terrorized, and as deeply as we believe in the principles of free speech and a free press, we could not in good conscience place the men and women who work at the *Phoenix* and its related companies in physical jeopardy."

Many American artists did not shy away from reacting to the Danish cartoon controversy. Wiley Miller's syndicated comic strip, *Non Sequitur*, presented a sidewalk artist who "finally achieves his goal to be the most feared man in the world," his placard advertising "Caricatures of Muhammad While You Wait!" Chip Bok in the *Akron Beacon Journal* depicted a CNN correspondent displaying one of the Danish cartoons featuring a pixilated head of Muhammad with a bomb in his turban, and a viewer observing, "Well, no wonder Muslims are upset. Muhammad looks like he's on acid." And Pat Oliphant in the *Washington Post* limned a meeting of The Deities Association gathered on a cloud, where various spiritual icons were laughing hysterically as one of them said, "Hey, Muhammad, take a look at this cartoon! They've got you being hijacked by Muslim extremists—it's a riot!"

However, the *Post* has since become somewhat cautious. In 2007, it was one of at least twenty-five newspapers that declined to publish a couple of Berkeley Breathed's *Opus* Sunday comic strips, afraid that his character Lola Granola, by dabbling in Islam and adopting its conservative dress code for women, could be offensive to Muslims. A week later, she dons a Burquini—a bathing suit that covers her entire body—in preparation for a visit to the beach, while her boyfriend, assuming that she'll be wearing a yellow polka-dot bikini, says in the final panel that this "is how we're gonna straighten out the world." Only, in the original, he doesn't say "the world," he says "the Middle East."

It seems safer to target America's leading misleaders. When George Bush and Dick Cheney appeared together before 9/11 commission members—in private and not under oath—they inspired several editorial cartoons around the country showing Cheney as a ventriloquist and Bush as his dummy. One caption read, "No wonder Cheney talks out of the side of his mouth." And no wonder that, when Bush had a colonoscopy, doctors discovered the fingerprints of Cheney's right hand on those five polyps. The polyps turned out to be benign, although the host was malignant.

THE DISNEYLAND MEMORIAL ORGY

In August 2008, thirty-two individuals—many wearing costumes of Disney characters such as Minnie Mouse, Snow White, Cinderella and Tinker Bell—were handcuffed and arrested outside Disneyland after an hourlong march from one of three Disney-owned hotels involved in a labor dispute. They were protesting Disney's proposal that makes health care unaffordable for hundreds of employees by creating a new class of part-time workers who would receive no sick or vacation pay and would not be given any holidays.

A week later, the *Los Angeles Times* published a long report about Mickey Mouse's possible copyright problem. This cute little rodent who became an intellectual property was now 80 years old, with a 97 percent recognition rate in America, overshadowing even Santa Claus. Brand experts estimate Mickey's value to the Disney empire at more than $3 billion.

The day after Walt Disney died in December 1966,

stock in his company rose one point and continued to ascend. The studio earned $100 million the next year. No wonder Disney once said, "I love Mickey Mouse more than any woman I've ever known." Now Disney was gone, but Mickey Mouse would continue to bask in his own immortality.

I asked a Disneyland spokesperson, "Was there any special ceremony when Walt Disney died?"

"No, we kept the park open. We felt that Mr. Disney would have wanted it that way."

"Well, wasn't there *any* official recognition of his passing?"

"We did fly the flag at half-mast for the rest of the month."

In the midst of Disneyland's recent fiftieth anniversary celebration, *DisneyLies.com* claimed to be serving 50 to 100 gigabytes a day of online imagery: a couple of newlyweds caught consummating their marriage on Tom Sawyer Island after dark; major nudity on Mr. Toad's Wild Ride; a virtual orgy on Pirates of the Caribbean; a steamy incident with a couple of cast members in the secret room at the top of the Matterhorn. Ah, but what about all those cartoon characters themselves?

There was a rumor that Disney's body had been frozen, but actually it was cremated. Somehow I had expected Mickey and Donald Duck and the whole gang to attend the funeral, with Goofy delivering the eulogy and the Seven Dwarfs serving as pallbearers. Disney's death occurred a few years after *Time* magazine's famous "God Is Dead" cover, and it occurred to me that Disney had served as the Intelligent Designer of that whole stable of imaginary characters now mourning in a state of suspended animation.

Disney had been *their* Creator, and he had repressed all their basic instincts, but now that he had departed, they could finally shed their cumulative inhibitions and participate together in an unspeakable Roman binge, to signify the crumbling of an empire. I contacted Wally Wood—who had illustrated the first piece I sold to *Mad* magazine, "If Comic Strip Characters Answered Those Little Ads in the Back of Magazines"—and without mentioning any specific details, I told him my general notion of a memorial orgy at Disneyland to be published in *The Realist*. He accepted the assignment and presented me with a magnificently degenerate montage.

Pluto was pissing on a portrait of Mickey Mouse, while the real, bedraggled Mickey was shooting up heroin with a hypodermic needle. His nephews were jerking off as they watched Goofy and Minnie Mouse fucking on a combination bed and cash register. The beams shining out from the Magic Castle were actually dollar signs. Dumbo the elephant was simultaneously flying and shitting on an infuriated Donald Duck. His nephews, Huey, Dewey and Louie, were staring at Daisy Duck's asshole as she watched the Seven Dwarfs groping Snow White. The Prince was snatching a peek up Cinderella's dress while trying a glass slipper on her foot. The Three Little Pigs were humping each other in a daisy chain. Jiminy Cricket leered as Tinker Bell did a striptease causing Pinocchio's nose to get longer.

Actually, Mickey Mouse had been a convict in a chain gang when he originally met Pluto. In World War II, Mickey's name was the password for the D-Day invasion. And Snow White warned military personnel about the dangers of venereal disease. In the Disneyland Memorial Orgy, although none of the characters' genitalia is shown,

Wood had nonetheless unleashed their collective libido and demystified an entire genre in the process.

When the May 1967 issue of *The Realist* was published, an anonymous group in Oakland published a flyer with our logo on top, reproducing a few sections of the Disneyland Memorial Orgy, captioned "Now on Sale at DeLauer's Book Store, Your East Bay Family News and Book Store," and distributed it in churches and elsewhere. In Baltimore, the Sherman News Agency distributed that issue with the centerspread removed. An employee told me that the Maryland Board of Censors had ordered this—that it was the only way *The Realist* could be sold in the state—though no such committee existed. Sherman's had merely taken what they considered to be a precaution. I was able to secure the missing pages and offered them free to any Baltimore reader who had purchased a partial magazine.

In Chicago, a bookstore owner and my distributor (Chuck Olin, who also ran an ice cream company) were charged with selling and distributing obscene material. Theoretically, the charges couldn't stick legally. The centerspread certainly didn't arouse anyone's prurient interest, a criterion for obscenity at the time. I imagined a prosecutor telling a jury how they might get horny—"Just look at what Goofy and Minnie Mouse are doing"—but even if it *did* arouse prurient interest, the rest of *The Realist* was certainly not (in the Supreme Court's language) *utterly* without redeeming social value.

However, a judge found the issue to be "obscene." The charge against the distributor was dismissed, based on his lack of knowledge of the contents. The ACLU sought a federal injunction restraining authorities from interfering in any way with local distribution of *The Realist*.

The Disneyland Memorial Orgy centerspread became so popular that I decided to publish it as a poster. A source at the Disney corporation told me that they considered a lawsuit but learned that *The Realist* had no real assets, and besides, why bother causing themselves any further public embarrassment? They took no action against me; never even ordered me to cease and desist. (They did sue the producer of a pirated Day-Glo version of the poster; the case was settled out of court.) Ultimately, the statute of limitations on me ran out. In 2005, I published a new, copyrighted, digitally colored edition (available at paulkrassner.com) of the originally black-and-white poster.

As artistic irreverence toward the Disney characters has continued to grow, attorneys for Walt Disney Productions have become busy filing lawsuits to stop the sale of such items, because their corporate client has worked "for many years to acquire the image of innocent delightfulness known and loved by people all over the world, particularly, but not only, by children," but now these characters are being shown in a "degrading, lewd, drug addictive, offensive and defaced" manner, some of them "in poses suggestive of a love-in." The lawyers stated, "Some of the cartoons portrayed by these people are pornographic," and complained about "copyright infringement and unfair competition."

In 1971, 60,000 copies of an underground comic book, *Air Pirate Funnies*, were distributed—an extension of the Disneyland Memorial Orgy concept in story form, complete with bawdy speech balloons. One panel showed Mickey Mouse explicitly performing oral sex on Minnie Mouse. He was saying, "Slup Slup Slup Slup Slup, *Gulp!*, Slup Slup," while she was responding, "Ahhh Ng Oh! Yas! Ohhh M!" The Disney empire sued Dan O'Neill, Bobby

London and the other cartoonists. One courtroom artist told me he planned to draw all the jurors with Mickey Mouse ears. In 1972, I was asked to submit a sworn deposition in the case. My statement read:

"I have been the editor and publisher since its inception in 1958 of *The Realist*, which has been described by *Library Journal* as 'the best satirical magazine now being published in America.' I have read volumes one and two of *Air Pirates*, and find that their contents remain loyal to the traditional values of legitimate parody. It is always a presumption in this form of humor that whatever institution is criticized is, by definition, strong enough to withstand being made fun of. If a myth could actually be harmed—in this case, Mickey Mouse and his imaginary friends—merely by suggesting 'imperfectibility,' well, that is the risk and the blessing of democracy.

"In order to communicate an irreverence toward the Walt Disney characters, the original form must be imitated to provide the most effective vehicle of reaching the consciousness of the audience and hopefully causing them to question the one-dimensional infallibility of Disney's fairytale world. For any government to imply otherwise would be to foster brainwashing. In São Paulo, Brazil, a city official in charge of a campaign to exterminate rats said that public support for the program was adversely affected by the popularity of Mickey Mouse among children. It is in the highest tradition of a free society to encourage the testing of conflicting ideas in an open marketplace; the comic books in question, therefore, are classic examples of artistic responsibility in action."

In 1975, the defendants were found guilty of copyright infringement. The judge ruled in Disney's favor and assessed $190,000 in damages. In 1978, the U.S. Court of Appeals upheld that decision, denying the cartoonists' defense that their parodies were "fair use" of copyrighted material and that they drew the Disney characters in more exact likenesses than necessary to get their point across. But the court stated that "The desire of a parodist to make the best parody must be balanced against the rights of the copyright owner and his original expression. The balance is struck at giving the parodist what is necessary to conjure up the original." In 1979, the Supreme Court let stand the lower court ruling. Yes, the highest court in the land had managed to uphold the honorable image of Goofy.

But the Disney folks weren't victorious in every case. The Center for Constitutional Rights represented the Chilean co-authors of *How to Read Donald Duck* in a battle with U.S. Customs, and won. There was a law stating that if material came in through Customs that officials thought violated an American copyright, they could freeze the material and force the importer to fight for its release. This book was a sociological analysis of the capitalist ethic in Disney comics, illustrated with hundreds of strips. The case was won by proving that the reprinting was necessary "fair use" in order to comment on them.

However, in 1983, Canadian artist Carl Chaplin created "Wishing On a Star" postcards for free distribution. They depicted Disneyland being blown up by a nuclear bomb. Disney lawyers threatened legal action, demanding possession of the postcards. Chaplin said that "If Uncle Walt were alive, he would know that I did the painting to point up the horror of what could happen to all of mankind in a nuclear war." (In 1945, Aldous Huxley went to work for Uncle Walt as a consultant on the filming of *Alice in*

Wonderland. There were rumors that Huxley had turned him on with magic mushrooms. ("If people would think more of fairies," said Disney a year later, "they would forget about the atom bomb.") Nevertheless, Chaplin turned over all the remaining postcards. The irony was that, as a result of the lawsuit, that image was sent over the UPI wire and seen by millions who would otherwise have remained unaware of its existence.

In 1989, on the same day that Disney stock jumped 6.375 points in active trading, their attorneys arranged to have white paint splashed over the "innocent delightfulness" of Disney characters on murals at three day-care centers in Florida. They were replaced by Yogi Bear, Fred Flintstone and Scooby Doo.

In 1992, Britain's official artist for the Persian Gulf war, John Keane, got in trouble for his painting in which Mickey Mouse appears on what looks like a toilet, with a shopping cart of antitank missiles nearby and a background of shattered palm trees. A spokesperson for Disney said they were considering possible copyright violations. The artist said that the idea came to him in Kuwait City, in a marina used by the Iraqis, where he found a Mickey Mouse amusement ride surrounded by feces.

And in 2008, Disney sued a home-based business for $1 million after a couple organized children's parties with imitation Eeyore and Tigger costumes. It was yet another Mickey Mouse decision.

THE PARTS LEFT OUT OF *BORAT*

There are a few private jokes in *Borat.* One, which might merely be an example of a low-budget flick, is that the same bedspread appears in three different hotel room scenes. Another is that the anti-Semitic protagonist from Kazakhstan occasionally speaks fluent Hebrew throughout the movie.

An Associated Press dispatch referred to him as a "Jew-fearing journalist" and stated: "In the end, it appeared that naked wrestling, toilet jokes and anti-Semitic satire hold universal appeal." In fact, Rob Eshman, editor of the *Jewish Journal*, confessed that he laughed so hard he spit out his gum. Moreover, the following excerpt from a review in *Jewish Week* was subsequently forwarded on the Internet by an anti-Semitic listserv:

"The first time I saw Borat I fell madly in love with him. For a journalist who writes about culture in a major Jewish newspaper, seeing this fictional, mustachioed, deeply offensive, thoroughly anti-Semitic man for the first time on HBO two years ago was more than entertainment. It was a clarion call. . . . Played with fierce doggedness by Israeli-born comedian Sacha Baron Cohen, Borat—supposedly a reporter from Kazakhstan who travels the United States asking his hapless interviewees the most unthinkable of questions—was that mythological beast that all young Jews secretly dream about, a character cool and commanding who puts, if only for a moment, all things Jewish at the cutting edge of popular culture."

Well, any movie that serves to unite Jews and anti-Semites can't be all bad. Certainly, both sides appreciate, for different reasons, Borat's explanation that the reason he and Azamat—his outstandingly obese "producer"—drive rather than fly across America in this documentary-style parody of a buddy movie is because he's scared that Jews would hijack their plane "like they did on 9/11."

(John Stauber, co-author of *Weapons of Mass Deception: The Uses of Propaganda in Bush's War on Iraq*, told me, "Skilled propagandists can plant gossip, and if it takes root and spreads successfully, it can serve a useful propaganda purpose. For instance, gossip has helped spread the false propaganda that Jews stayed home from work at the World Trade Center on 9/11 because they were warned of the attacks in advance. This is an outrageous lie, but that has not stopped it from being spread and believed by those predisposed to so believe.")

To be fair, though, the anti-Semitic listserv—whose editor hasn't laughed out loud so much since he saw *Schindler's List*—also called the Jewish critic "hypocritical."

Sacha can be compared to several other performers. Like Lenny Bruce, his sense of irreverence enables him to communicate from the villain's perspective. Lenny, in his boldest satirical critique, perceived reality from Adolf Eichmann's point of view. Like Sarah Silverman, Sacha can make light of rape, advising his father, the hometown rapist, to keep his standards high by raping only humans. Sarah pretends in *The Aristocrats* that she was once raped by show-biz legend Joe Franklin. Like Robin Williams, Sacha becomes the characters he plays so thoroughly it almost seems as if he loses his own center in the process. Like Chevy Chase, he's a practitioner of pratfalls. Like Andy Kaufman, his sense of absurdity can stretch the patience of an audience beyond its ordinary limits.

Sacha is the contemporary version of a professional prankster, the latest stage in the evolution of a tradition, from *Candid Camera* to Tom Green to *Punked* to correspondents on *The Daily Show*. He stays in character with the determination of a salmon swimming upstream, blurring the line between courage and foolhardiness, just as Stephen Colbert did so uncompromisingly at the White House Correspondents' Dinner.

On the *Tonight* show, as Borat, he outdid Mel Gibson's drunken outburst, informing Jay Leno that "The Jews were responsible for the end of the dinosaur period." Later, he leaned across the next guest, Martha Stewart, grabbed Leno's finger in his fist and said, "My sister. This tight."

Sacha's schtick depends on tricking people into becoming his theatrical props, people who tolerate his outrageousness in order to be hospitable and not hurt his feelings. In the process, they reveal the state of their own humanity, for better or worse.

Of course, everybody sees any film through the filter of their own particular subjectivity, so it's logical that my friend Nick Kazan, a screenwriter who treats his craft with great respect, would say about Sacha, "His commitment to his character is absolute and admirable, but I wish there'd been a little more narrative focus. A better plot. I wish it hadn't been just the same as the TV show."

Through Kazan, I was able to find a source in the industry who gave me a montage of outtakes from the raw footage of *Borat* on condition that it neither be auctioned on eBay nor posted on YouTube. I was given permission to describe some of those scenes that remain on the cutting-room floor—a concept, incidentally, that has been laid to rest in the Outdated Metaphors Graveyard by the grace of digital editing.

However, permission has *not* been granted concerning the details of a specific scene showing fraternity boys getting drunk in a bar with the producers, due to their lawsuit claiming that they were duped into making racist and sexist remarks, "behavior that they otherwise would not have engaged in." (This news inspired mention of "the Mel Gibson defense" as instantly as Britney Spears's divorce inspired mention of her former husband Kevin Federline as "Fed-Ex.")

The scene following the one showing three feminists walking out of Borat's blatantly misogynist interview is left out, wherein the producers persuade them to return, only to be subjected to the unrelenting Borat's request that they remove their tops. One of them, artist Linda Stein, has since drawn a small penis on his thong, because, "as he exposed people, he should be able to take what he gives."

Another segment—ostensibly to contrast a county jail in California with the brutal conditions of a Kazakhstan prison—was passed over *entirely* because the film crew was ordered out of the premises when Borat pretended he was being arrested and said, "I like-a this place. Very nice. When you make all the mens do a pyramid, can I be on top?"

In another scene that was omitted from the final product—if only because it would have interfered with the basic premise, a continuity of innocence, whether faked or real, of Sacha and his participant-victims alike—Pamela Anderson is forewarned that, at a bookstore signing, when he asks her to marry him, he will thrust a Kazakh wedding bag over her head, an act that would otherwise have terrorized her. Plus a scene at Malibu Beach in which Borat—wearing his skimpy jockstrap-style chartreuse bathing suit—chases Pamela and finally tackles her. Also appearing only in the rough cut was footage of her then-husband, musician Kid Rock, pacing back and forth, looking extremely agitatated.

A few scenes were excised because their inclusion would have resulted in an NC17 rating for *Borat* instead of an R. One scene involving his handing a plastic bag filled with his fresh feces to the hostess at a dinner party made the cut, but the preceding scene—Borat actually defecating, as seen from the inside the toilet—was deleted for that rating reason, but it was also considered too artsy-fartsy.

There was a hysterical scene on a porn set where Borat wouldn't have sex with an actress because her crotch was shaved. To solve the problem, he cuts locks of his own hair off and pastes them to her crotch. But this scene was eliminated, not only because of ratings-fear, but also because it would have been inconsistent with the scene where he tells a car dealer he wants to buy a car that will be "a pussy magnet" for women who "shave down there," and the dealer suggests a Corvette or a Hummer.

In the naked wrestling scene with the blubbery yet agile Azamat, a black rectangle would have to be superimposed on Borat's penis in postproduction because of his erection, which was not a stage direction in the skillfully choreographed script.

My favorite missing scene, which *does* allow the revelation of his penis because it's flaccid—acceptable under the rules of the ratings game—takes place in the office of a Beverly Hills plastic surgeon. Borat is there to discuss having a foreskin sewn back on because he doesn't want Pamela Anderson to think he's Jewish on their honeymoon night. After he drops his pants and fishnet underwear, he points to his penis and says, "I have seen on the televisions you will draw lines in magic marker, that is correct?"

The doctor pauses. He looks puzzled. Then suddenly he realizes something, snaps his fingers and shouts, "Wait! You're Ali G! You're Ali G! You used to be on HBO! You're Ali G!" The crew's attempt to stifle their laughter fails, but

Sacha remains in Borat-character. "Aha," he says, "so you recognize it, yes?"

Ironically, the more famous Sacha becomes, the less likely his schtick will work. His cover has been blown, even if he has not.

GETTING HIGH DOWN UNDER

In 1988, I was booked to perform at Lincoln Center, sharing the stage with poet Allen Ginsberg and performance artist Karen Finley, whose infamous reputation for shoving a sweet potato up her ass preceded her appearance. Lenny Bruce had taught me by example about the magic of an opening line that intuitively articulates the consciousness of an audience.

"Well," I began, "Allen Ginsberg is very disappointed. He thought that Karen Finley was gonna shove a sweet potato up *his* ass."

Eighteen years later, in May 2006, I was looking forward to seeing Karen again. She had written a novella, *George and Martha*, about a one-night stand between George Bush and Martha Stewart, and I was scheduled to be on a panel about satire at the Sydney Writers Festival with her and Andy Borowitz, recipient of the "first-ever National Press Club Award for Humor" (unless, of course, that's just his idea of a joke).

I flew to Los Angeles, then began a sixteen-hour flight to Australia, only to make a U-turn two hours into the trip because of a mechanical problem resulting in cabin pressure too low for the plane to fly at the necessary altitude. Customer Relations told me that hotel rooms were unavailable, but I got two meal vouchers that were good at any restaurant in the airport except Wolfgang Puck's and McDonald's. I spent twenty-seven hours in the L.A. airport, alternating between attempts to sleep and dragging my luggage around. In the bathroom, it stood in front of the urinal next to the one I was using.

Plus I caught up on my packet of research material. I learned that in some ways, the United States and Australia are similar—they are the only two countries in the world to reject the Kyoto Protocol. And in other ways, they're different—in the United States, seven states, including Alabama and Texas, have banned the sale of sex toys including vibrators, whereas in Australia, prostitutes, strippers and lap dancers can claim deductions for sex toys, condoms, lubricants, gels and oils.

The next night, Tuesday, May 23, I left again on the same flight, arriving on the morning of Thursday, May 25, airport- and jet-lagged. After shaving and showering in my hotel room, it was time to leave for a panel on obscenity and censorship at the Sydney Theater. Later that afternoon, I performed at a cabaret, and a member of the audience kindly slipped me a generous package of pot. I immediately bought Tally-Ho rolling papers and a lighter with a smiley face, returned to the hotel, got stoned, ate dinner, watched CNN and fell asleep.

When I woke up, Friday's *Sydney Morning Herald* was waiting outside my door. In a front-page review, I was described as the "star entertainer on obscenity. . . . [Krassner] is about to test religious tolerance with a sex scene he is writing between Jesus and Mary Magdalene. She screams, 'Oh, God!' And He replies, 'Yes?'" In 1962, Lenny Bruce had been kicked out of Australia for obscenity and blasphemy. Now I felt as if I had avenged him.

Australia still has a bizarre puritanical streak, though. In December 2008, a man was convicted of possessing child porn for having lewd images of *The Simpsons* on his hard drive. He could have been sentenced to prison for up to ten years, but instead he was fined $3,000 and placed on two years' probation. He appealed the decision, arguing that fictional cartoon characters could not be considered people, as they "plainly and deliberately" departed from the human form. But the judge found that while *The Simpsons* characters had hands with four fingers and their faces were "markedly and deliberately different to those of any possible human being," the mere fact that that they were not realistic representations of human beings did not mean that they couldn't be considered people.

Anyway, except for a few media appearances, that Friday at the Sydney Writers Festival was my day off. It was always fun to hear a distinguished interviewer carefully enunciate the title of my book, *One Hand Jerking*. One interviewer would only state the subtitle, *Reports From an Investigative Satirist*. I had the whole afternoon free to explore the wharf. After a bowl of pumpkin soup, I was drawn toward an area in the park by the sound of a voice on the public address system.

This was May 26, which happened to be the date of an annual commemoration called "Sorry Day." On that date in 1997, Australians were shocked by an official report that detailed the anguishing evidence of some 30,000 indigenous and mixed-race Aboriginal children having been kidnapped by the government, from 1869 into the early 1970s, and forcing them to live with white families. These people are known as part of "The Stolen Generations." There was nothing in the media before or after this poignant anniversary, but that evening I talked about it during a radio interview.

"Terrorism," I concluded, "begins at home."

I also brought up the subject during the satire panel. I was wearing a Sorry Day T-shirt that acknowledged "Australia's Hidden Agenda: Assimilation, Genocide, What's Not Talked About." When I bought the T-shirt, I asked what sizes it came in. The answer was, "Large, Extra Large, and Extra Extra Large." I told the audience that "I felt like I was in Starbucks. Talk about assimilation. . . ."

Around fifteen years ago, I met an American who owned a ranch in Australia. He told me about an Aboriginal child he knew who slept on a bed made of leaves and twigs and who went to a school where they had two computers, run by a generator. He had already hacked into the system at MIT, and his next experiment would be the Pentagon. Now he was a young man, and since I was visiting Australia, I had hoped to track him down and find out what he was up to, but unfortunately it was too late—I had to return to the United States.

I left Sydney on Monday afternoon, May 29, and arrived in Los Angeles on Monday morning, May 29. I had given away the remainder of my marijuana stash, but I kept the lighter and the pack of rolling papers. At a specific point almost near the end of that pack, there was an ungummed, maroon rolling paper to remind customers, "When you've got 10 to go, just say Tally-Ho."

In November 2007, the Aboriginal people celebrated the defeat of Minister for Indigenous Affairs Mal Brough, architect of the government's invasions of Aboriginal communities leading up to the election, just as they had previously celebrated the defeat of Prime Minister John

Howard, who had refused, year after year, to simply say to them, "I'm sorry."

In 2008, the Australian government finally apologized to its victims.

In 2009, an indigenous leader and director of the Tasmanian Aboriginal Centre complained that "Aboriginal people, and especially members of the Stolen Generations, are probably worse off. . . ."

HARRY SHEARER HEARS VOICES

Harry Shearer became an actor when he was 7 years old, at the urging of his piano teacher. When he was a kid on the *Jack Benny Show*, as the cast was doing a read-through, there was one line in the script where, he told me, "I just got it in my mind to do it with a slight Brooklyn accent, and when I did that, Benny just started howling, banging the table and laughing." That moment was an auspicious omen of Shearer's future career.

Foremost among his many talents is an uncanny ability to mimic with satirical precision the voices, mannerisms and points of view of countless public figures—entertainers, politicians, news anchors—on his radio program, *Le Show*, which completed its twenty-fifth year on the air in late 2008. It has been broadcast every Sunday morning on KCRW in Santa Monica ("From the edge of America, from the home of the homeless") and syndicated to around 100 stations in this country, plus one in Berlin, NPR in Europe, an audio feed on Japan's cable system, and American Forces Radio.

For more than a quarter century, Shearer has never been paid for doing *Le Show*, but what about the perks?

"Well, one of the advantages of doing weekly radio shows is that you tend to forget them as soon as they're done," he told me. "The great part, since gaining Internet coverage, is hearing feedback from listeners in places like Japan and Africa, where this broadcast would never be heard on terrestrial radio. But the real highlight, from a life standpoint, has to be when I had a chance meeting on the street, near the newsstand just off Melrose, with somebody who was a fan of the radio show, and whose then-column in the then–*LA Reader* I was a fan of. It was Matt Groening, and that meeting led to a little remunerative gig in the Murdochian vineyards."

Shearer was referring, of course, to *The Simpsons*, on which he performs voiceovers of several cartoon personalities. Since he does both Mr. Burns and his assistant, Smithers, I asked, "When you're taping *The Simpsons*, do you sometimes just stand there and talk to yourself?"

"Yes, and that happens a lot," he said. "When Hank [Azaria] plays Apu and Chief Wiggum, he'll talk to himself, and when Dan [Castellaneta] plays Homer and his dad, he'll talk to himself."

One of the voices he has done on *Le Show* is TV journalist Dan Rather. When the Museum of Radio and Television honored Rather, he personally invited Shearer to attend. Shearer wanted to discuss issues, but Rather preferred to talk about *Spinal Tap*, the classic rock 'n' roll mockumentary where Shearer played Derek Smalls, the bassist in the band.

Ironically, the band was put together and existed only for the sake of the movie, yet ended up going on tour. During their London appearance, Shearer entered the brunch place at the hotel where they were staying—still dressed as his character, with fake hair extensions but a real beard—and he was awe-stricken by a gifted vocalist, Judith Owen. Eventually they got married, and they now divide their time between Santa Monica and New Orleans. Sometimes when she performs at a club, Shearer accompanies her on the electric bass. And in keeping with his eclectic taste in music and his keen sense of nepotism, he often plays songs from her albums on *Le Show*.

Shearer always presents a few "copyrighted" features on his program. I won a bet with Nancy that they're not *really* copyrighted, and perhaps as a result of that bet, he introduced "Tales of Airport Security," where he reads listeners' accounts of such misadventures, as "a copyrighted feature of this broadcast, and when I say that, of course I am lying. That's full disclosure, ladies and gentlemen."

Another "copyrighted feature"—"If it ain't copyrighted," Shearer admits, "who knows the difference?"—is "Apologies of the Week," ranging from the creator of a comic strip, *Get Fuzzy*, apologizing for suggesting that Pittsburth smells bad, to the president of Serbia apologizing for evil committed during the war in Bosnia; from Brazil's government apologizing to the country's senior citizens for forcing them to show up at Social Security offices to prove they're not dead, to Burger King apologizing to a woman who was ordered by a franchise employee to stop breast-feeding her baby or leave, because it made a customer uncomfortable.

"Yeah," Shearer observed, "it brings you down seeing somebody eating better than you at a Burger King."

In the tradition of Lenny Bruce, he plays all the characters in audio-theatrical sketches that serve as a vehicle for his incisive humor. He has frequently presented phone conversations between George Bush and his father, taking the part of both and capturing the nuances of each. In his own voice, alluding to Bush's crusade to stamp out global terrorism, Shearer has observed, "It's like the war on drugs. It's a totally metaphorical war in which some people get killed. I expect the Partnership for a Terrorist Free America to start soon."

But how will Shearer handle Barack Obama?

"I think there's going to be something sadly funny about the collision/intersection between the sky-high hopes and expectations of his supporters with the sky-high mountain of crap left on his desk by his predecessors," he says. "I'm still learning his speech pattern, but there's something about the way he emphasizes certain words, especially the ones at the ends of sentences, that gives the aura of decisiveness whether there's anything decisive being said or not."

I asked Shearer, a dedicated news junkie (including satellite feeds), about his philosophy of comedy.

"Comedy is good," he said, "reality is better."

And his all-time favorite example?

"Well, I would say my object of idolatry in that regard would be the tape of Richard Nixon just before he makes his resignation speech. You can't beat that. [*In Nixon's voice*] 'Ollie there, he's always trying to take another picture of me, but he's always trying to get one of me picking my nose. You wouldn't do that, would you, Ollie? That's enough now.' Just the lunacy of him kidding around with this crew that you can actually see on the tape—they don't know what to make of this, and a guy who entered a field where one of the primary qualifications is the ability to make charming small talk, and then at this climactic penultimate moment in Nixon's fall, what does he choose to do but walk in and make that insane small talk? That to me is one of the great choices ever."

THE POWER OF LAUGHTER

I spent a weekend in September 2007 at the eleventh annual Earthdance celebration, a global festival for peace held in northern California, uniting with more than 250 locations in fifty countries, providing a wide variety of live music, workshops, speakers, inspiration and a worldwide sense of community.

On Saturday, I was among a large group of men and women participating in the International Elders Forum. Each one had six minutes to share their wisdom with an overflowing crowd in the huge Electronica Dome. A Native American, David Rain of the Blackfoot tribe, would play the flute after five minutes of talk as a signal that there was one minute left.

When my turn came, I began, "Whatever wisdom I have to share is in the form of comic relief, but just remember, if you don't laugh you're only helping the terrorists." After seven minutes, I still didn't hear any notes from the flute, so I decided to pass the microphone on to the next person.

On Sunday afternoon, David told me that he had been laughing so hard he simply couldn't play his flute. He tried again and again, yet the best he could do was spit into it. Of course, this was gratifying feedback to a stand-up satirist, but over lunch our conversation became deadly serious.

In November 2006, he had wanted to sell a piece of equipment, and a man who saw the ad invited him to his converted garage apartment. There, David was told to help himself to a soda from the refrigerator, which he did. When he turned around, four men—biker/skinhead/Aryan-Nation types—burst through the door and attacked him with 2.5-inch metal pipes, first striking him on the forehead, then beating and kicking him while calling him a "dog" and a "prairie nigger."

He tried unsuccessfully to defend himself and finally dove out the first-floor window, bouncing off a table and a car before landing on the ground. He pounded on somebody's door—yelling "9-1-1!"—then collapsed in a puddle of blood. He regained consciousness in a hospital where he got forty stitches for a cracked cranium and a head brace for his broken neck. His shoulder and hand were also injured. He was rescued by a friend and stayed at her home to heal. He could no longer do physical work, but she helped him open a small business.

Two weeks after the incident, on Thanksgiving Eve, police arrested David for missing a court date on a traffic violation. He had missed the date because he was unconscious in the hospital at the time. In the Sonoma County jail, guards kicked him, removed his head brace, refused him all medical attention, placed him in solitary confinement, forced him to sleep on a concrete bed without a mattress and did not allow him to shower for six days. They eventually brought him to court, chained to a wheelchair.

After he was released on probation, the district attorney demanded that David testify against the skinheads. Knowing the nature of the Aryan gang, he immediately expressed concerns about his safety, regardless of what his testimony might be. A couple of months later, the DA agreed to place him in a witness protection program. It turned out to be at the Pink Flamingo, a hotel in Santa Rosa, the same city in which he was attacked.

On the third day, he walked out of the hotel and saw a crowd of bikers and skinheads hanging around. Not knowing they were there for a tattoo convention, he panicked, returned to his nonsmoking room and smoked a cigarette. The alarm went off. For that offense, he was evicted from the hotel and taken out of the witness protection program. The DA was angry. She made it very clear to him that "We have ways of making you testify."

The day before the trial, David was arrested again, on the way to the Indian Health Center, for driving with a suspended license. Again, he was denied medical attention, his head brace was removed, and he was thrown into solitary confinement. A week later, he was again brought into court chained to a wheelchair—unbathed, "looking like a wild Indian," he says—and threatened with three years in jail. The DA was in the courtroom at his sentencing, powwowing directly with the judge.

Immediately before the sentencing, David's friend stood up and asked to speak out on his behalf, since his court-appointed lawyer had done so little to defend him. With the bailiff bearing down on her and contempt of court looming, the judge surprisingly agreed to let her talk. She stated how jailing David was "cruel and unusual punishment, because he would have to be placed in solitary confinement throughout his incarceration in order to avoid any contact with Aryan gang members, due to his status as a hate-crime victim.

"He was in violation of driving with a suspended license only because he couldn't afford to pay the fines; his injuries prevented him from being able to work in his chosen field to earn the money to pay those fines. Was driving with a suspended license actually worth three years of anyone's life, or was there another agenda lurking in the courtroom that needed such leverage to pressure David into testifying against the assailants? Was it justice to, in effect, condemn him for the heinous crime of poverty?"

The judge weighed the case and the next day released David on probation, warning him not to drive. Almost a year later, the DA was still hounding him by phone and subpoena, putting his life in danger by coercing him to testify. And where was Victims Assistance during all this horror? A Victim Witness Advocate told David, "I can't help you. You're on probation. Our hands are tied."

Since David was a victim, he didn't have the right to a public defender. He was due to appear in court the week after Thanksgiving, 2007. He planned to say that he would not testify because, "If concern for my safety is not addressed, I could die." He expected to be charged with contempt and, once again, to be put in solitary confinement. In the hope of extricating him from this profane injustice of criminalizing a victim, I was able to find a couple of attorneys who could give him helpful advice.

Ultimately, he didn't have to testify.

I'm grateful to be in a position to communicate the details of this nightmare, none of which I would've known had David been able to play his flute after five minutes of laughter.

2.

THE WAR ON SOME PEOPLE WHO USE SOME DRUGS

THE BALLAD OF TOMMY CHONG

Jonathan Shapiro, a writer and executive producer of the Fox TV series, *Justice*, reviewed Tommy Chong's book, *The I Chong: Meditations From the Joint*, for the *Los Angeles Times*. Shapiro wrote:

"Being incarcerated for resisting imperial power or because of one's sexual preference or getting sent to the gulag for dissenting opinions are searing human tragedies that inspired brave acts of artistic resistance. Selling bongs over state lines just doesn't carry the same moral weight."

Hey, Jonny boy, whoa! You'd better buy a new state-of-the-art apocryphal scale if you're going to measure for comparison the moral weight of prison sentences.

On February 24, 2003, Tommy Chong was among fifty-five people who were arrested in raids across the country as a culmination of the DEA's Operation Pipe Dreams, named after one of Cheech and Chong's stoner movies. Agents forced their way through the door of his home at six o'clock that morning, with automatic weapons drawn.

Chong was the only one who served time—nine months at a federal prison—and paid a $20,000 fine, not to mention the $103,000 that was seized when he got busted.

The reason he became an exception and received such punishment was precisely *because* of his "dissenting opinions" and "artistic resistance." It simply would not have happened otherwise.

They wanted to get him really bad. Traditionally, local law enforcement has discretion to decide what priority should be given to prosecuting cases involving drug paraphernalia. Because both Pennsylvania and Ohio make that a top priority, the DEA chose to open a decoy head shop in Pennsylvania. Four times in one year, these stingmeisters tried to make an online purchase of a pipe autographed by Chong, but his Nice Dreams Enterprises would not fill any orders coming from either of those two states.

However, a request from a different return address easily passed through the apparently fake firewall of a new employee. In an appearance at the Peppertree Bookstore in Palm Springs, California, Chong said that he suspected the employee was sent to infiltrate his company. I wanted to know why Chong suspected that. He responded that it was a very strong suspicion, based on the fact that the employee left the company a couple of days before the bust, giving no reason.

In a deal with the authorities, Chong agreed to plead guilty in exchange for his wife and son not being indicted. Ironically, he was sentenced on September 11, 2003, the second anniversary of *real* terrorist attacks, rather than a business run by an actor in such Cheech and Chong movies as *Up in Smoke* and, more recently, a recurring role on a popular sitcom, *That '70s Show*, where he continued to play the part of a dedicated pot smoker.

The prosecutor, U.S. Attorney Mary Beth Buchanan—ignoring all relevance of the First Amendment in favor of her professional career—had the audacity to introduce Chong's fictional character in the courtroom as evidence of his "frivolous" attitude toward the enforcement of drug laws. Chong said this was "like jailing all of the *Police Academy* people for making fun of cops." Furthermore, he had joked with reporters about putting this criminal case in his next movie with Cheech. The prosecution insisted that such a comment indicated that Chong was making light of the case and might exploit it for money.

Behind bars, Chong said, "I'm a doper comedian, and I'm in here because I made a stupid joke about the bongs being the only weapons of mass destruction that the Bush administration had found." Half Scottish-Irish, half Chinese and raised in Canada, he points out that "when I became an American citizen, I took a vow to uphold the Constitution of the United States. Doing anything less than exercising my right of free speech in defense of pot and against its prohibition would be a violation of my vow."

So listen, Jonathan, for a future episode of *Justice*, how about considering a story line revealing the basic *in*justice of arresting 830,000 individuals every year for the "crime" of possessing marijuana? It may not get you high, but hopefully your consciousness will be raised in the process.

As for prosecutor Buchanan, *her* career had been inadvertently boosted by the terrorist attacks in 2001 when a United Airlines plane crashed inside her jurisdiction, (sixty miles southeast of Pittsburgh), catapulted her to prominence in the law-enforcement community and enabled her to instigate the yearlong undercover sting. Three days after 9/11, she became the first woman and the youngest person in Pennsylvania history ever to be named a U.S. attorney, and for her first major operation, she chose Chong as her priority target because *his* career had "glamorized" the use of marijuana.

In March 2009, she prosecuted the owners of a Northridge, California, company that sold videos depicting deviant sexual conduct, charging the couple with conspiracy to distribute obscene material, after a six-year battle over whether the First Amendment protects such material, which included scenes of simulated rape. They finally pleaded guilty. Once again, Buchanan had brought a case in western Pennsylvania, this time because the area's "community standards"—which, according to the U.S. Supreme Court, govern what's obscene—are more conservative than California's.

Meanwhile, the cruel absurdity of anti-paraphernalia laws continues to be underscored by such creative substitutes as apples, soda cans, toilet-paper cardboard tubes with aluminum foil, tweezers used as roach clips, and don't forget those plain old regular *tobacco* pipes.

In Fulton, Kentucky, police investigating a marijuana-smoking complaint found pot burning on a backyard grill with a large fan on the other side of the house, sucking the smoke throughout the home—in effect, said the police chief, "turning the house into a large marijuana bong." Seize it immediately!

BARACK OBAMA AND THE POT LAWS

During a debate in the Democratic presidential primary campaign, MSNBC moderator Tim Russert asked the candidates who opposed decriminalization of marijuana to raise their hands. Barack Obama hesitantly raised his hand halfway before quickly lowering it again.

However, in January 2004, when Obama was running for the Senate, he told Illinois college students that he supported eliminating criminal penalties for marijuana use or possession.

"I think the war on drugs has been a failure, and I think we need to rethink and decriminalize our marijuana laws," he said during a debate at Northwestern University. "But I'm not somebody who believes in legalization of marijuana." Was Obama now having a time-travel debate with *himself*?

When the *Washington Times* confronted Obama with that statement on a video of the 2004 debate, his campaign offered two explanations in less than twenty-four hours. First, a spokesperson said that Obama had "always" supported decriminalizing marijuana, that he misunderstood the question when he raised his hand, and reiterated Obama's opposition to full legalization, adding that an Obama administration would "review drug sentences to see where we can be smarter on crime and reduce the blind and counterproductive sentencing to nonviolent offenders."

But after the *Times* posted the video on its Web site, the Obama campaign made a quick U-turn and declared that he does *not* support eliminating criminal penalties for marijuana possession and use—thereby rejecting both legalization *and* decriminalization. What exactly is the difference? The definitions, according to *Pot Culture: The A-Z Guide to Stoner Language & Life*, by Shirley Halperin and Steve Bloom:

"**Decriminalization**: When laws governing marijuana are changed to reduce the penalties for possession of small quantities (usually below an ounce) to non-criminal status. The first state to decriminalize was Oregon in 1973, followed by California, New York, Ohio, Nebraska, Minnesota, Colorado, Mississippi, Alaska, North Carolina and Maine.

"**Legalization**: The complete repeal of marijuana prohibition and removal of all criminal penalties for its use, sale, transport and cultivation. The Netherlands is the only country in the world with such a policy."

Ron Fisher at NORML told me, "Decriminalization is the elimination of criminal penalties for the possession of marijuana, usually by replacing them with a fine (similar to a speeding ticket). Full legalization is a more complex issue that involves U.S. treaties as well as the law. Legalization would be characterized by taxation and regulation of marijuana. This is NORML's ultimate goal, but we work for decrim in the meantime for the sake of the 830,000 Americans arrested on cannabis charges each year."

Indeed, a CNN/Time-Warner poll shows that 76 percent of Americans agree with Obama's original position, not to mention the 48 million who smoked pot in 2007.

The *Progressive Review* quotes an old classmate of Obama explaining the meaning of *chooming*: "That's what we called smoking marijuana. To 'choom' meant to get high, to smoke pot. I never heard the word used anywhere else, but Punahou kids had access to the very best pot available." He and Obama were in the group of students who smoked marijuana, and members of the choom group did so both on and off campus. The irony is that, had Obama been arrested then, he might never have been able to run successfully for the presidency.

Review publisher Sam Smith tells a story that underscores the hypocrisy of the political pandering that continues to allow unjust laws to turn tokers into criminals: "Early in the Clinton administration your editor had dinner with, among others, a high White House official—a lawyer. The conversation turned to marijuana. The lawyer said that numerous staffers had asked how they should respond to FBI queries on the matter. The official's reply was that they should remember that they would only be in the White House for a short while but the FBI files would be there forever. And what if friends or relatives actually saw them using pot? The White House lawyer's response: 'If you can't look an FBI agent straight in the eye and tell him they were wrong, you don't belong here.'"

During the campaign, Obama promised that he would end the federal raids on dispensaries, or, as he later worded it for the *San Francisco Chronicle*, he would curb federal enforcement on state medical marijuana suppliers.

A few days before Obama selected Joe Biden as his running mate, Tommy Chong, in an interview with the *Washington Post*, was asked what the average citizen could do to further the cause of decriminalization.

Chong replied: "Check out the people you're voting for. For instance, Joseph Biden comes off as a liberal Democrat, but he's the one who authored the bill that put me in jail. He wrote the law against shipping drug paraphernalia through the mail—which could be anything from a pipe to a clip or cigarette papers."

Before becoming vice president, Biden, who coined the term "drug czar," also sponsored the Rave Act, which targets music events where drug use is supposedly prevalent. As for medical marijuana, he said, "We have not devoted nearly enough science or time to deal with the pain management and chronic pain management that exists. There's got to be a better answer than marijuana."

You mean like prescription drugs, which result in 100,000 deaths a year while marijuana has caused none?

Anthropologists of the future will surely look back upon these times as incredibly barbaric. Medical marijuana is already legal in thirteen states, yet it's prohibited—and trumped—by federal law. Shortly after Obama's inauguration, the DEA raided several medical marijuana dispensaries in and around Los Angeles, but in March 2009, his new U.S. Attorney General, Eric Holder, announced that the Justice Department now has no plans to prosecute dispensaries in those states where it's legal.

States' rights . . . it's not just for racists any more.

BONG HITS 4 JESUS

The U.S. Supreme Court sucks so badly that it finally turned itself inside out. In 2007, their outrageous 5-to-4 ruling made it acceptable to suspend a high school student for the off-campus act of holding a 14-foot banner reading "Bong Hits 4 Jesus." That harmless bit of incongruity became a federal case ending with a dangerous precedent for suppressing free speech.

Chief Justice John Roberts agreed with the school principal that "the banner would be interpreted by those viewing it as promoting illegal drug use, and that interpretation is plainly a reasonable one." What a ton of bullshit. Justices Samuel Alito and Anthony Kennedy voted with him, but also stated that their decision doesn't address "political or social issues such as the wisdom of the war on drugs or of legalized marijuana for medical use." Ironically, this is the same Supreme Court that upheld the illegality of medical marijuana by falsely denying the existence of positive research.

Studies have concluded that cannabis is effective for relieving muscle spasms and chronic pain in AIDS patients. The miracle weed can both increase hunger in HIV patients and suppress hunger to fight obesity. It can help those with glaucoma, Alzheimer's, asthma, hepatitis, diabetes, epilepsy, osteoporosis, arthritis, insomnia, sleep apnea, migraine headaches, scoliosis, hypertension, depression, shingles, PMS, menopause, Parkinson's disease and multiple sclerosis. Cannabinoids can inhibit the proliferation of cancer cell lines, including breast, prostate, colon, pancreatic and brain cancer.

But cynical critics treat the legalization of medical marijuana as though it was intended to be a gateway leading to legalization of nonmedical marijuana. So this is really about the war on pleasure. I once asked the late Peter McWilliams—a leading activist in the medical marijuana movement who suffered from cancer and AIDS—"Would you agree with Dennis Peron, the co-author of Proposition 215 [California's medical marijuana referendum], who says—not as a joke—that *all* use of marijuana is medical?"

"In the general sense that everything we do for our health—both curative and preventative—is medical, I'd agree," he replied. "Even a perfectly healthy person who smokes pot once a month purely for its euphoric effects could be said to be doing so to prevent becoming ill, in the sense that people take vitamin C every day to prevent becoming ill, for I believe that euphoria is both healing and health-maintaining. . . .

"While I was using marijuana to treat my nausea, I can't tell you how much I missed getting high. Although I'd smoke it several times a day, the average high school student was getting high more times a month than I was. That's because after the first month, I never got high, and I really enjoy marijuana's high. Simply put, recreational marijuana you use to get high; medical marijuana you use to get by."

The *New York Times* editorialized, "Although there are other prescriptions that are designed to relieve pain and nausea, and there is concern about the health effects of smoking marijuana, there are some truly ill people who find peace only that way." But those "other prescriptions" are pushed by the pharmaceutical industry, which spent a record-breaking $155 million to lobby the government from 2005 to mid-2006. In fact, the Partnership For a Drug-Free America was originally founded and funded by the tobacco, alcohol and pharmaceutical companies.

The priorities are insane. Cigarettes cause 1,200 deaths every day in the United States alone. Nearly 2,000 young people under the age of 18 become smokers every day in America. And yet, although the World Health Organization spent three years working out an agreement with 171 countries to prevent the spread of smoking-related diseases, particularly in the developing world, the United States opposed the treaty, including the minimum age of 18 for sales to minors. Around the globe, tobacco now kills almost five million people a year. Within a generation, WHO predicts, the premature death toll will reach ten million a year.

Whereas, with marijuana, the worst that can happen is maybe you'll have a severe case of the munchies and conduct a midnight raid of your refrigerator. In the past forty years, 20 million Americans were arrested for violating anti-marijuana laws, primarily for simple possession. As long as any government can arbitrarily decide which drugs are legal and which are not, anyone behind bars for a drug offense is a political prisoner.

As for "concern about the health effects of smoking marijuana," it was reported at the 2005 meeting of the International Cannabinoid Research Society that smoking marijuana—"even heavy long-term use"—does not cause cancer of the lung, upper airways or esophagus. As for recent claims of psychosis, the rate of psychosis has remained unchanged since 1950, while the rate of marijuana use has increased 10,000 percent since then.

Former drug czar John Walters insists that pot growers are "violent criminal terrorists who wouldn't hesitate to help other terrorists get into the country with the aim of causing mass casualties." But syndicated columnist Clarence Page—referring to WAMM, the Wo/Men's Alliance for Medical Marijuana—has written about the DEA raiding "a legitimate health cooperative that was treating more than 200 patients, some of them terminally ill, in Santa Cruz [California]. Snatching medicine out of the hands of seriously ill patients sounds like terrorism to me. In this case it was federally sponsored and taxpayer-financed."

WAMM, founded by Valerie and Mike Corral, has been helping people dying of cancer and AIDS for fifteen years. Learning that such patients couldn't afford the high cost of marijuana, WAMM established a communal garden where medicine is grown for patients who have a doctor's recommendation; they may take what they need and give what they can, even if that is nothing.

The late Robert Anton Wilson, a prolific countercultural author, told me, "I never thought I would become another WAMM patient. My post-polio syndrome had been a minor nuisance until then. Suddenly, two years ago, it flared up into blazing pain. My doctor recommended marijuana and named WAMM as the safest and most legal source. By then I think I was on the edge of suicide—the pain had become like a permanent abscessed tooth in the leg. Nobody can or should endure that."

After the DEA raided WAMM's garden and arrested its founders, outraged Santa Cruz city and county officials sponsored WAMM's medical marijuana give-away on the steps of City Hall and joined WAMM's lawsuit against the DEA, the U.S. Attorney General and the Office of National Drug Control Policy. WAMM was considered the most likely organization to ultimately sway the Supreme Court. According to Federal Judge Jeremy Fogel, "WAMM is the gold standard of the medical marijuana movement."

Meanwhile, what ever happened to Joseph Frederick? He was the 18-year-old student who, when the Olympic torch passed through Juneau, Alaska in 2002, seized upon the opportunity to hold up that banner, "Bong Hits 4 Jesus." He went on to learn Mandarin and teach English in China. He's proud that he stood up for his rights, with the aid of the ACLU, but regrets "the bad precedent set" by the Supreme Court ruling. However, his case was settled at the state level in November 2008, winning him $45,000 and forcing the school to hold a forum on free speech.

If only that banner had read "Bong Hits 4 WAMM," then, by the Supreme Court's own language—that their decision did not address "political or social issues such as the wisdom of the war on drugs or of legalized marijuana for medical use"—the "Bong Hits 4 Jesus" student would not have been punished. He would've been protected by the First Amendment, because *blasphemy* is protected by the First Amendment. But the prejudiced Supreme Court Justices rationalized that "Bong Hits 4 Jesus" was "promoting illegal drug use," even though such promotion is *also* protected by the First Amendment.

I'll smoke to that.

WAS MOSES TRIPPING?

So now I have a new theological question: What exactly was Moses tripping on while hallucinating that he was parting the Red Sea? After all, Benny Shanon, who teaches cognitive psychology at the Hebrew University of Jerusalem, theorizes in the journal of philosophy *Time and Mind* that Moses was simultaneously high on Mount Sinai and high on psychedelics when he heard God delivering the Ten Commandments.

"The thunder, lightning and blaring of a trumpet which the Book of Exodus says emanated from Mount Sinai could just have been the imaginings of a people in an altered state of awareness," he writes. "In advanced forms of *ayahuasca* inebriation, the seeing of light is accompanied by profound religious and spiritual feelings."

Concoctions based on the bark of the acacia tree, which is frequently mentioned in the Bible, contain the same molecules as those found in the vines of the powerful psychotropic plant from which the liquid ayahuasca is prepared. Professor Shanon has himself ingested ayahuasca during a religious ceremony in Brazil's Amazon forest.

His article came out of a lecture he gave at a conference organized a few years ago by Chris Bennett, who tells me, "It would be interesting to know if anyone has produced a working ayahuasca-like preparation from the local mid-Easter flora and fauna. As it now stands, the information regarding cannabis, or *keneh bosem*, which is regarded as the Hebrew word for pot by a growing number of linguists and etymologists, is much more substantial and believable. What is more interesting about Shanon's theory is that it helps demonstrate the possibility of both shamanism and the use of psychoactive substances in the Bible."

However, Daniel Sieradski, who has been researching the subject of Jews and drugs for six years, claims that "while in Israel, Benny Shanon was one of the individuals I met on two separate occasions during the course of my research, and he basically lifted his 'Moses was high' theory from me, which I shared with him. Though I'm quite pleased that he's bringing attention to these ideas, and that he makes them 'his own' by adding his own spin to the subject—I can't deny that Shanon has his own body of work to draw from, nor can I even necessarily fault him if he doesn't recall our conversation—although it still kind of sucks, missing the boat on publishing the theory before he did. Ah, bitter lemons. Anyway, I believe the Israelites were likely consuming psilocybin."

Sieradski proceeds to tell me the story of the manna: "After the Jews left Egypt and were wandering in the desert, they're starving and complaining and pleading to

God for food, and so there's this miracle of manna, which has traditionally been viewed in mainstream religious discourse as this magical bread that falls out of the sky and it keeps the people fed for the duration of their wandering in the wilderness before entering the Holy Land. What manna seems to be is a hallucinogen." He speaks of "mass hallucination . . . seeing sounds and hearing colors." From my own experience, I recall tasting ice cream in my toes while on LSD. In any case, Shanon suggested on Israeli public radio that Moses was also on drugs when he saw the Burning Bush.

High Times editor Steven Hager says, "I've long believed the Burning Bush story was about cannabis, and that is what most Rastafarians believe. When the New Testament was constructed by the Roman Empire, all references to psychedelics and cannabis may have been removed, because those were probably considered secrets for an elite priest class. The only references that survive are from the Old Testament (*keneh bosem*, burning bush), which was already published and not under their control."

Aided by this new perspective, let us step into the time machine and travel to ancient civilizations and witness certain aspects of religion as history instead of a fairy tale.

Here we see Jesus and his disciples in the midst of an Ecstasy party, embracing each other as they slow-dance to the music of Mistress Magdalene and the Merry Maidens. Oh, look, Judas is French-kissing Jesus.

Going further back in time, we find Joseph plucking the magic mushrooms out of a pile of his donkey's manure, and then sharing them with the dove that somehow impregnated his wife, the one and only Virgin Mary.

Even further back, we come upon Moses, thoroughly stoned on the DMT that he has been snorting as he begins to set the original Ten Commandments in stone:

"Thou shalt not bogart that joint."

"Thou shalt not dose anyone with acid."

"Thou shalt not dilute cocaine with baby powder."

"Thou shalt not watch TV while using mescaline."

"Thou shalt not steal from thy parents' prescription medicines."

Moses stops to check his spelling, then speaks to God: "Some day, oh Lord, these commandments will be posted on every citizen's door."

HOOKAHS ON PARADE

You might want to read this while listening to "White Rabbit" by Jefferson Airplane: "Tell 'em a hookah-smoking caterpillar has given you the call." I smoked a hookah for the first time at a Middle Eastern restaurant in Cleveland. I liked it. And passing the many-tentacled water pipe around the dinner table enhanced our sense of community.

The sweet-flavored combination of apple and peach was tasty, plus I got a pleasant kind of dizziness. This was a legal high, because there was no pot in it. I was smoking a blend of 70 percent fruit, honey, herbs, flowers and molasses and 30 percent tobacco. I've never been a cigarette smoker, but Dr. Eugene Schoenfeld—who, as Dr. *Hip*-pocrates, wrote a syndicated column for the underground press in the '60s and who now specializes in the causes and effects of addiction—explains why I got stoned:

"Continuously and deeply inhaling cooled, flavorful tobacco mixtures will cause the user to experience a very relaxed, elated mood. And if the user is traditionally a nonsmoker, they will experience an even more concentrated feeling of relaxation, because their system is not used to the effects of inhaled smoke. A non–tobacco user will experience an altered mental state."

However, the World Health Organization warns that using a hookah to smoke tobacco is "not a safe alternative to cigarette smoking" and that the rising popularity of hookahs is partly due to "unfounded assumptions" of safety and misleading commercial marketing.

Not to mention the fact that, according to Scott Graber—sales manager of the Austin-based *hookah-shisha.com*, one of the country's top retailers of hookah products—"Media exposure to the Middle East is the biggest factor in growth. Servicemen and women returning from Iraq have embraced it. And it is seen as the cool social thing to do among college students."

Although cigarette smoking is prohibited in California bars and restaurants, hookah bars are exempt. There's even a hookah-smoking place in Hollywood where you have to know the password to get in. But the question remains, will a control-freak government eventually crack down on hookahs simply because they can be *considered* drug paraphernalia?

Since 1990, federal law has made drug-paraphernalia violators subject to RICO—Racketeer Influenced and Corrupt Organization—and money-laundering charges. Jerry Clark and Kathy Fiedler ran a head shop called Daydreams that turned into a nightmare when they were raided by the DEA, U.S. Postal Inspectors, local police and sheriff's deputies. The RICO Act was used against them, so they faced ten to twelve years behind bars.

Under federal law, merely manufacturing, distributing or selling nontraditional pipes is enough evidence to be found guilty of paraphernalia offenses. Authorities insist that companies can no longer protect themselves by posting signs or Internet warnings that indicate that their products are intended for tobacco use only. So I hereby call to the attention of law enforcement officials an invitation to "Come and have fun at our Hookah Party Fundraiser to support Iraq Veterans Against the War"—obviously a group of Rush Limbaugh's "phony soldiers"—and to an article in *Time* magazine which states:

"At cafes around UCLA and in college towns across the country, students are passing around the hookah, the ancient Middle Eastern water pipe filled with sweetened tobacco. In the past couple of years, the hookah has been resurrected in youth-oriented coffeehouses, restaurants and bars. The Gypsy Cafe serves up as many as 200 hookahs at $10 a pipe. At the Habibi, smokers have rented more than 500 hookahs in a night. Young patrons of the lounges agree that part of the hookah's charm lies in its illicit associations. 'It looks illegal,' says a Gypsy customer, 18, with a grin, sucking on his hookah with the insouciance of the blue caterpillar in *Alice in Wonderland*, 'but it's not.'"

And finally, just in case you guys at the DEA missed it, *High Times* magazine presented *Late Night* host Conan O'Brien with the beautiful Stoney Bong Award for comedy, and he kept it. Hurry, it's still in his possession. He said that he planned to use it as a glass-eye holder, but that doesn't matter, you can still bust him.

GOT VOMIT?

Ethan Nadelmann, head of the Drug Policy Alliance, has said that "No one should be punished for what they put into their bodies." Of course, he's referring to punishment by law enforcement, but the punishment can also come from the insides of a curious experimenter. It's the risk of freedom.

Besides the usual suspects, among the substances that have been eaten, smoked, snorted or sniffed in order to get high are morning glory seeds, cough medicine, mace (the food seasoning), rug cleaner, dramamine, kanemanol, nutmeg, banana skins and flagyl (intended for vaginal infections).

According to an article in the journal *Pediatrics*, there's an online drug encyclopedia that gets 250,000 clicks a day. The Web site lists hundreds of mind-altering chemicals, herbs and plants, plus thousands of posts by youthful users about their own particular experiences.

Every two years, the California Department of Education conducts a survey with the state attorney general's office. In October 2006, the results of their latest study of 10,638 students in 113 middle and high schools revealed that 15 percent of eleventh-graders, 9 percent of ninth-graders and 4 percent of seventh-graders have been using pharmaceutical drugs without a prescription.

Guess where they find them: at parties in a game called "pharming," which involves the use of a bowl of randomly collected pills. Researcher Rodney Skager states, "young people come in and grab the ones that look pretty and take them. This is obviously a really dangerous practice. I have no idea how common it is." And they find them in their parents' medicine cabinets, where teenagers have been snatching legal drugs like OxyContin and Vicodin even before trying marijuana or alcohol.

Kathryn Jett, director of the California Department of Alcohol and Drug Programs, said, "We will be targeting our research now on the issue of prescription drug use to make certain that this does not continue to increase. As a parent, you need to be vigilant as to where those drugs are kept. Or if you have painkillers and don't need them, you need to dispose of them. If you have painkillers and you do need them, count them—know how many there are."

The *New England Journal of Medicine* reported the case of 18-year-old twin sisters in France. Their mysterious symptoms were scaly skin on their legs and hands; they were also unsteady and mentally sluggish. The cause? A bag of mothballs, which was stashed in the the drawer of a night table in the hospital room, and discovered by a cleaning lady. The girls had been using the mothballs to get high, inhaling air from the bag for about ten minutes a day because classmates had recommended it.

The sicker of the two had also been chewing half a mothball a day for two months. She told the doctors that she continued to use the mothballs during her hospitalization "because she thought her symptoms were not related to her habit." It took her six months to fully recover. Her sister had only been "bagging" for a few weeks, and recovered in three months.

Although radio talk show host Michael Jackson has said, "Anything that can make vomit pretty is certainly worth taking," referring to psychedelics, *Prison Legal News* discloses what is perhaps the most bizarre example of self-intoxication: drinking drug-laced vomit. Prisoners at the Pine Grove Correctional Center in Canada have been drinking each other's drug-laced vomit to get high. In fact, one inmate died there as a result of this practice.

Sonia Faith Keepness was found dead in her cell at the women's prison from ingesting a lethal combination of methadone and librium. She had swallowed two hits of methadone-laced vomit and taken four pills of librium. Two fellow prisoners admitted that after receiving their daily dose of methadone, they returned to their cells and regurgitated into a container for Keepness. They have been charged with drug trafficking, along with a third woman who provided the librium.

Methadone is a narcotic painkiller that is prescribed for drug addicts because it alleviates the unpleasant symptoms associated with the withdrawal from heroin. At the Pine Grove infirmary, prisoners in the methadone program receive their daily dose of the narcotic—ironically, itself addictive—mixed with orange juice. They routinely traded their methadone-laced vomit in return for certain favors from other prisoners.

"Methadone is a powerful drug," an inmate pointed out. "They wanted to get high, and they were desperate enough to drink someone's puke."

Prisoners are now required to remain under observation for one hour after drinking their daily dose.

Finally, in September 2007, a Collier County, Florida, sheriff's *Information Bulletin* issued a warning about "Jenkem," a new drug made from raw sewage—a mixture of fermented fecal matter and urine—and included photos of the brown liquid in a bottle and a teenager inhaling the gas produced by the mixture from a balloon in order to achieve a "euphoric high similar to ingesting cocaine but with strong hallucinations of times past. The high has been described by subjects as a feeling of being 'out of it' and talking to dead people. All subjects who used the Jenkem disliked the taste of sewage in their mouth and the fact that the taste continued for several days." The *Bulletin* reported that Jenkem "is now a popular drug in American schools." Word began to spread. By November, a drug counselor on KXAN in Austin was advising parents, "If there is a very funky smell or odor, ask. . . ."

Could it have been a hoax? Someone named "Pickwick" took credit on the Internet for staging that photo and confessed that his Jenkem was just dough rolled in Nutella hazelnut chocolate spread. But then a DEA offical told the *Washington Post*, "There are people in America trying [Jenkem]." Was that true or had a hoax transmuted into an urban legend? Certainly it's true that in Zambia, many thousands of street children have been resorting to Jenkem for over a decade. "Initially, they used to get it from the sewer, but they make it anywhere," said John Zulu, director of the Ministry of Sport, Youth and Child Development in Zambia. "They say it keeps them warm and makes them fearless."

In any case, *snopes.com*, the Bible of Rumor Research, has not found any evidence to substantiate the original sheriff's *Information Bulletin* claim.

HOW MAGIC ARE YOUR MUSHROOMS?

There I stood, in San Francisco on April Fools' Day 1995, with my feet spread apart and my arms outstretched against the side of a car. As I was being frisked by a police officer, I realized that he was facing the back of my *Mad* magazine jacket, the face of Alfred E. Neuman smiling at him and saying, "What, me worry?" And, indeed, this cop *was* worried. He asked if I had anything sharp in my pockets. "Because," he explained, "I'm gonna get very mad if I get stuck," obviously referring to a hypodermic needle.

"No," I said, "there's only a pen in this pocket"—gesturing toward the left with my head—"and keys in that one."

When he saw the contents of the baggie that he removed from my pocket, he asked a rhetorical question—"So you like mushrooms, huh?"—with such hostility that it kept reverberating inside my head. I hadn't done anything that would harm somebody else. This was simply an authority figure's need to control. But control what? My pleasure? Or was it deeper than that?

◆ ◆ ◆

In 2008, the *Journal of Psychopharmacology* published the results of a daylong experiment involving psilocybin, also known as "magic mushrooms." Although this psychedelic has been used for centuries in religous ceremonies, it's still illegal. The study, which took place at a Johns Hopkins University laboratory, was funded by the National Institute on Drug Abuse and involved thirty-six male and female volunteers.

Fourteen months later, 64 percent still felt at least a moderate increase in well-being or life satisfaction, in terms of creativity, self-confidence, flexibility and optimism; 61 percent reported at least a moderate change of behavior in positive ways; 58 percent rated the session as one of the five most personally meaningful experiences of their lives; 67 percent said that the drug had produced one of the five most spiritually significant experiences they'd ever had. Many spoke of being more sensitive, tolerant, loving and compassionate. According to one participant, "I feel more centered in who I am and what I'm doing. I don't seem to have those self-doubts like I used to have." She referred to "taking off . . . being lifted up." Then came "brilliant colors and beautiful patterns, just stunningly gorgeous—more intense than normal reality," she added. "I feel much more grounded and that we are all connected. There was this sense of relief and joy and ecstasy when my heart was opened."

Head researcher Roland Griffiths stated, "This is a truly remarkable finding. Rarely in psychological research do we see such persistently positive reports from a single event in a laboratory. This gives credence to the claims that the mystical-type experiences some people have during hallucinogen sessions may help patients suffering from cancer-related anxiety or depression and may serve as a potential treatment for drug dependence."

Rick Doblin, founder of the Multidisciplinary Association for Psychedelic Studies (MAPS), has been able to break through "the forty-year-long bad trip" that he and other researchers have faced in dealing with the negative fallout from the introduction of LSD and other psychedelic compounds in the mid-1960s. He describes this four-decade intellectual Dark Age as being characterized by "enormous fear and misinformation and a vested interest in exaggerated stories about drugs to keep prohibition alive."

Charles Shaw points out on *AlterNet* that "What was lost in all the derision and urban myths about LSD and other psychedelic compounds like *ayahuasca*, peyote, psilocybin and *iboga*—plant medicines thousands of years old—was the fact that they are miraculously powerful medicines, with the ability to effectively treat, and in some cases, cure some of the most debilitating illnesses and disorders plaguing humanity: addiction, obsessive-compulsive disorder, Post-Traumatic Stress Disorder, and migraine and cluster headaches. They are also effectve palliatives for the sick and dying. . . ."

Referring to Doblin's pioneer work, he writes, "Western governments had to ask themselves what was more important to them: their irrational and erroneous drug propaganda, or the possibility that the millions of lives they had devasted by war, violence and iniquitous economic policies might actually be repaired. In this, the seeds of a psychedelic renaissance were planted."

◆ ◆ ◆

As for my psilocybin bust, I got off with a $100 fine and nothing on my permanent record. But I finally understood what that police officer had meant when he sarcastically snarled, "So you like mushrooms, huh?" What was his *actual* message? Back through eons of ancestors, this cop was continuing a never-ending attempt to maintain the status quo. He had unintentionally revealed the true nature of the threat he perceived. What he had really said to me was, "So you like the evolution of human consciousness, huh?"

"Well, yeah, when you put it like that, sure I do. I like it a whole lot."

3.

UNDER THE COUNTERCULTURE

HIPPIES ON THE HITLER CHANNEL

The History Channel recently presented a two-hour documentary titled *Hippies*. Co-sponsored by the American Association of Retired People, it was a crude attempt by AARP—considered by some to be a front for the insurance and pharmaceutical industries—to reach the aging babyboomer market, although the program turned out to be a blatant slur on countercultural history.

I had been interviewed for a few hours and was dismayed to see that the one quote they used—beginning "It was fun"—immediately followed a scene of police indiscriminately beating young demonstrators at an antiwar rally. Violence galore. You'd think you were watching *The Sopranos*. Or maybe the evening news. I asked a few fellow participants for their reactions.

• Roz Payne, DVD producer, *What We Want, What We Believe: Black Panther Library*: "Throughout the show, I was yelling to my daughter 'This is shit!' I had spent about three hours being filmed, but I was cut and chopped into one-sentence bits. My first line was, 'I took LSD at UCLA'—they left out that LSD was part of the Psychology Department research—it was legal. I felt I was chopped into little sound bites."

- Ken Babbs, sidekick of Ken Kesey and the roving band of Merry Pranksters: "The show sucked. Zane [Kesey's son] said he was ashamed to have had anything to do with it. That picture of a bus, calling it the Ken Kesey Prankster bus—I suppose it doesn't do any good to point out that it is not Further but someone else's bus, for as time goes on, whatever anyone portrays as reality works just fine."

- Carolyn Garcia, former wife of Jerry Garcia, also known as Mountain Girl from the Merry Pranksters: "Could more negative terms be found? I must have turned it off five times. If I had known the bias of the piece, I would have abstained. I hate being blamed for Manson and riots and people bleeding. What a nasty raft of crap. Well, what can one do about this bash-fest? Peter Coyote was obviously forced at gunpoint to read the script."

"I didn't see the piece," Coyote told me, "but I've sure gotten shit about it. The last thing that we ought to be doing is getting uptight with one another or ourselves over the fraudulence and trickery of other people. I was taken by these guys, and so were a lot of other people. The guy that produced it was a quisling, and I fought with him all through the recording and made him make many changes, but I couldn't control how he would cut and edit. We've all been misquoted before, and used for other people's agendas. This film is just not a big deal. At the end of the day, the Grateful Dead and the Diggers and the counterculture have already changed American culture irrevocably. There is no place in the United States today where you cannot find organic food, environmental movements, alternative spiritual practices, alternative medical practices, peace movements. . . ."

In addition to narrating *Hippies*, Coyote had been interviewed by Lance Miccio, who also interviewed Mountain Girl, Wavy Gravy, Country Joe McDonald, Roz Payne, Ken Babbs, Martin Lee, Lenore Kandel, Fito de la Parra, Buddy Miles, Elsa Marley and myself, among others.

Somebody else interviewed the right-wingers—including Ed Meese, former attorney general, and Rick Brookhiser, senior editor at the *National Review*—who were given way too much time to spout their disdain for hippies. According to the editor, Tracey Connor, she was given a script, and she had to find footage to fit that script; then later more script was added, and she said she had to change shots, but then it was too long so she had to cut. But the question is, why was Miccio's work maneuvered into such a hodge-podge of prejudicial propaganda?

"What can I say?" he asked me. "*Hippies* by the Hitler Channel. It was not what I had hoped for. I feel like the guy in *Pulp Fiction* who said it best: 'We went into this with the best of intentions.' Then Samuel Jackson shoots him in the knee. The executive producer [and co-writer], Scott Reda, saved money by not having a director. He fired anyone who objected to his cost-effective vision of what the hippies were about. Although he was alive in the '60s, I think he did two '50s and went right into the '70s. I supplied him with enough real firsthand information from those who were there, but they chose to ignore or manipulate it into a dirty story about dirty hippies. I am sorry to all of you who allowed me into your life so the History Channel could present you in such a slanted, misunderstood view. I am so pissed off that I was a pawn in this bullshit documentary. My deepest apologies to all."

In Reda's hometown paper in Easton, Pennsylvania, the *Express-Times*, Tony Nauroth wrote:

"The show was spawned from a book he stumbled across—*Hippie* by Barry Miles. 'At first the film was going to mimic the book,' Reda says—'very light, from 1965 to 1970 or '71, but the network kept saying, *We know about that, we know about that, we know about that.* Literally at our fifteenth draft, they said, *Tell us something we don't know.*' Through intense below-the-skin research, Reda emerged with the film's dark direction—fewer flowers and more drugs; lost children fumbling their way around the predatory jungle that the Mecca of hippie life, Haight-Ashbury, had become."

However, we can be grateful to other voices for presenting the positive side. *San Francisco Chronicle* columnist Mark Morford:

"The hippies had it right all along. All this hot enthusiasm for healing the planet and eating whole foods and avoiding chemicals and working with nature and developing the self? Came from the hippies. Alternative health? Hippies. Green cotton? Hippies. Reclaimed wood? Recycling? Humane treatment of animals? Medical pot? Alternative energy? Natural childbirth? Non-GMA seeds? It came from the granola types (who, of course, absorbed much of it from ancient cultures), from the alternative worldviews, from the underground and the sidelines and from far off the goddamn grid, and it's about time the media, the politicians, the culture as a whole sent out a big, wet, hemp-covered apology."

Michael Simmons, who has written more than 125 articles about marijuana, told me, "When I had a medical procedure earlier this week, they made me fill out a form that asked what ethnicity I am. I wrote 'Hippie-American.'"

And Stephen Gaskin wrote in an introduction to the revised version of his 1970 book, *Monday Night Class*: "I consider myself to be an ethnic hippie. By that I mean that the ethnicity I grew up with was such a white bread, skim milk, gringo experience that it wasn't satisfying for me. It had no moxie. Now, being a hippie, that's another thing. I feel like the Sioux feel about being from the Lakota Nation. I feel like Mario Cuomo feels about being Italian. It makes me feel close with Jews and Rastafarians. I have a tribe, too. I know that the hippies were preceded by the beatniks, the bohemians, the freethinkers, Voltaire and so on, back to Socrates and Buddha, but the wave of revolution that spoke to me was the hippies. And rock 'n' roll lights my soul and gives a beat to the revolution."

The spirit of that revolution continues to flourish. The sense of community is celebrated at such annual events as the Rainbow Gathering, Burning Man, Earthdance, and the Starwood Neo-Pagan Festival. Countercultural notions that were nurtured four decades ago are still blossoming into mainstream consciousness. And all the remaining psychedelic relics I know have not stopped serving as agents of change.

STRANGE BEDFELLOWS AMONG THE YIPPIES

Sixties-bashing is in fashion again. Columnist Gregory Rodriguez writes, "The excesses of the 1960s gave rise to a conservative counterrevolution. Abbie Hoffman begat Ronald Reagan; Timothy Leary begat John Ashcroft. Just as the counterculture railed against free-market capitalism and traditional morality, a resurgent political conservatism—which would exhibit its own excesses—emerged to preserve and defend them. The '60s bequeathed us the culture wars, and the divisions it wrought became the organizing principles of national politics."

Sixties-bashing reared its psychedelic head during one of the Republican "debates" in October 2007. John McCain said that Hillary Clinton and other Democrats would raise taxes, and he singled out a proposal she made for federal funding of a museum commemorating the 1969 Woodstock festival. "I'm sure it was a cultural and pharmaceutical event," he said, adding, in reference to having been a prisoner of war during the Vietnam conflict, "I was tied up at the time." And Mike Huckabee, speaking of Clinton's health care plan, said, "When all the old hippies find out that they get free drugs, just wait. . . ."

But there was one particular week in 2006 when 1960s-bashing had a print-media field day.

As a co-founder of the Yippies with Abbie Hoffman and Jerry Rubin, I observed how they were able to manipulate the media to further their antiwar mission. If you gave good quote, you got free publicity. Furthermore, in a tactic borrowed from the CIA, if you manipulated an event covered by the media, no direct manipulation of the media was necessary. If the Yippies presented newsworthy street theater, then the press manipulated itself.

Fortunately or unfortunately, depending on your agenda, that kind of behavior has a way of backfiring. And so I was both amused and annoyed by an item in the "Inside the List" column by Dwight Garner in the August 13 edition of the *New York Sunday Times Book Review*. He wrote:

"Thomas Ricks, senior Pentagon correspondent for the *Washington Post*, has a book on the hardcover nonfiction list this week—his *Fiasco: The American Military Adventure in Iraq* (Penguin Press) makes its debut at No. 1. Ricks's book got a boost from strong reviews and from appearances on both *The Charlie Rose Show* and NPR's *Fresh Air*, where Terry Gross interviewed him on two successive days. Ricks is a fleet, vivid writer, but he's also got a gift for radio. On *Fresh Air*, he filled the air with analogies that were funny, sad and apt, sometimes all at once. George Bush and his team were like '60s radicals. ('They really were going to, kind of, "groove on the rubble," as Jerry Rubin used to say. They were going to tear it down and see what happened.')"

Ricks told me, "I actually think that, more than anyone realizes, Bush was formed in reaction to the '60s, and that is what I had in mind when I said (and wrote) that."

"Has it come to this?" asks anthropologist and Yippie archivist Samuel Leff. "With the Iraq war now an obvious catastrophe, Ricks is comparing the Bush gang's mindless destructiveness to '60s radicals like Rubin? John Dean correctly compares the Bush and Nixon White House as regimes much more like fascism than democracy. The destruction of democracy, then and now, emanated from a radical Oval Office. Richard Nixon put thugs to work breaking the noses of protest leaders, from Abbie Hoffman (successful) to Daniel Ellsberg (unsuccessful)."

From the Richard Nixon tapes:

NIXON: "Aren't the Chicago Seven all Jews? Davis is a Jew, you know.
CHIEF OF STAFF H.R. HALDEMAN: "I don't think Davis is."
NIXON: "Hoffman, Hoffman's a Jew."
HALDEMAN: "Abbie Hoffman is. . . ."
NIXON: "About half of these are Jews."

Anthony Summers' book on Nixon, *The Arrogance of Power*, includes a photo of Hoffman with his nose bandaged, being taken away from his apartment by a detective. The caption reads, "In 1971, Nixon and Haldeman discussed using Teamster thugs to beat up antiwar demonstrators and smash some noses. Two days earlier, they had broken the nose of Abbie Hoffman. 'They got him,' Haldeman now told the president."

In the August 17 issue of the *Los Angeles Times*, linguist Geoffrey Nunberg—in an op-ed piece titled "Who Are You Calling a Fascist?"—wrote:

"In the mouths of the neocons, 'fascist' is just an evocative label for people who are fanatical, intolerant and generally creepy. In fact, that was pretty much what the word stood for among the 1960s radicals, who used it as a one-size-fits-all epithet for the Nixon administration, American capitalism, the police, reserved concert seating and all other varieties of social control that disinclined them to work on Maggie's farm no more. . . . Time was when right-wingers called the ACLU a bunch of communist sympathizers. Now Bill O'Reilly labels the group and others as fascist, with a cavalier disregard for the word's meaning that would have done Jerry Rubin proud."

Leff comments that, "If Nunberg had been thrown down the stairs, as Rubin was, by the New York City Tactical Police Force—a Waffen SS–type goon squad of especially large men in uniform—who raided his apartment looking for drugs on secret orders from the FBI, Nunberg would have less 'cavalier disregard' for using Rubin's name in the same breath as the authoritarian fascist personality of Bill O'Reilly. He is as much like Jerry Rubin as Slobodan Milosevic is like Che Guevara."

On August 20, Frank Rich wrote in his *New York Times* column:

"The hyperbole that has greeted the [Ned] Lamont [Democratic primaries] victory in some quarters is far more revealing than the victory itself. In 2006, the tired Rove strategy of equating any Democratic politician's opposition to the Iraq war with cut-and-run defeatism in the war on terror looks desperate. The Republicans are protesting too much, methinks. A former Greenwich selectman like Mr. Lamont isn't easily slimed as a reincarnation of Abbie Hoffman or an ally of Osama bin Laden."

Yeah, right. It was bad enough that a brainwashed American public would even believe Bush administration propaganda that Saddam Hussein and Osama bin Laden were married in Massachusetts and then adopted a Chinese baby. But Hoffman was a defendant in the Chicago Conspiracy Trial, and bin Laden was behind the 9/11 terrorist attacks. Now, however, in the guise of history, they were retroactively paired. Abbie and Osama, together again.

In 1967, when I told Abbie that he was the first one who made me laugh since Lenny Bruce died the previous year, Abbie said, "Really? He was my god." The combination of satirical irreverence and sense of justice that Lenny and Abbie shared was the essence of the Yippies—a term I coined to describe a phenomenon that already existed: an organic coalition of stoned hippies and political activists who engaged in such actions as throwing money on the floor of the New York Stock Exchange, then explaining to reporters the meaning of that symbolism.

Folksinger Phil Ochs summed it up: "A demonstration should turn you on, not turn you off." So when journalists link the Yippies with misleading bedfellows, at best it's careless shorthand; at worst it's deliberate demonization. Osama bin Laden wanted an airplane to crash into the Pentagon. Abbie Hoffman merely wanted to levitate it.

THE PARTS LEFT OUT OF *CHICAGO 10*

In 1967, Abbie Hoffman, his wife Anita and I took a work-vacation in Florida, renting a little house on stilts in Ramrod Key. We had planned to see *The Professionals*. "That's my favorite movie," Abbie said. "Burt Lancaster and Lee Marvin develop this tight bond while they're both fighting in the Mexican revolution, then they drift apart." But it was playing too far away, and a hurricane was brewing, so instead we saw the Dino Di Laurentiis version of *The Bible*. Driving home in the rain and wind, we debated the implications of Abraham being prepared to slay his son because God told him to. I dismissed this as blind obedience. Abbie praised it as revolutionary trust.

This was the week before Christmas. We had bought a small tree and spray-painted it with canned snow. We were tripping on LSD as the hurricane reached full force. "Hey,"

Abbie yelled over the roar, "this is pretty powerful fuckin' acid!" We watched Lyndon Johnson on a black-and-white TV set, although LBJ was purple-and-orange. His huge head was sculpted into Mount Rushmore. "I am not going to be so pudding-headed as to stop our half of the war," he was saying, and the heads of the other presidents were all snickering and covering their mouths with their hands so they wouldn't laugh out loud. This was the precise moment we acknowledged that we'd be going to the Democratic convention in August to protest the Vietnam War. I called Dick Gregory in Chicago, since it was his city we were planning to "invade." He told me that he had decided to run for president, and he wanted to know if I thought Bob Dylan would make a good vice president.

"Oh, sure," I said, "but to tell you the truth, I don't think Dylan would ever get involved in electoral politics."

I also called Jerry Rubin in New York to arrange for a meeting when we returned. The conspiracy was beginning.

On the afternoon of December 31, several activist friends gathered at the Hoffmans' Lower East Side apartment, smoking Colombian marijuana and planning for Chicago. Our fantasy was to counter the convention of death with a festival of life. While the Democrats would present politicians giving speeches at the convention center, we would present rock bands playing in the park. There would be booths with information about drugs and alternatives to the draft.

We sought to utilize the media as an organizing tool, but we needed a name so that journalists could have a "who" for their "who-what-when-where-and-why" lead paragraph. An appropriate word to signify the radicalization of hippies. I came up with Yippie to describe a phenomenon that already existed, an organic coalition of psychedelic hippies and political activists. In the process of cross-fertilization at civil rights rallies and antiwar demonstrations, we had come to share an awareness that there was a linear connection between putting kids in prison for smoking pot in this country and burning them to death with napalm on the other side of the planet. It was the ultimate extension of dehumanization.

And so we held a press conference. A reporter asked me, "What happens to the Yippies when the Vietnam War ends?" I replied, "We'll do what the March of Dimes did when a cure for polio was discovered; we'll just switch to birth defects." But our nefarious scheme worked. The headline in the *Chicago Sun-Times* read, "Yipes! The Yippies Are Coming!" What would later happen at the convention led to the infamous trial for conspiring to cross state lines to foment riot. As an unindicted co-conspirator, I felt like a disc jockey who hadn't been offered payola.

Flash ahead to 2005. I got a letter from *Vanity Fair* editor Graydon Carter, and then a call from Brett Morgen, director of *The Kid Stays in the Picture*. They were co-producing a documentary about the antiwar movement of the 1960s. It would have no narrator and no talking heads, only archival footage and animated reenactments based on actual events and transcriptions of trial testimony. However, Allen Ginsberg floating a few feet above the floor while he chants can be construed as cartoonic license.

Brett invited me to write four specific animated scenes:

1. "Birth of the Yippies"
This would include the hurricane, the meeting and the press conference. Excerpt:

[*The house is shaking mightily on its stilts.* ABBIE, ANITA *and* PAUL *are looking out the window through wildly waving curtains as the house feels like it will be swept away. Books are falling off the shelf. Newspapers are swirling around the room.*]

ABBIE [*screaming*]: "This whole house is gonna blow straight out to Cuba! [*lightning strikes*] We're coming, Fidel! [*sound of thunder*] Sock it to us, God!"

2. "Got Permit?"

We meet with Chicago deputy mayor David Stahl, attempting to get a permit for the revolution—that is, permits to sleep in the park, set up a sound system and march to the convention center. Excerpt:

STAHL: "C'mon, tell me, what do you guys *really* plan to do in Chicago?"

PAUL: "Did you ever see that movie, *Wild in the Streets?* [*A thought balloon shows the image of a group of teenagers dumping LSD into the water supply.*]"

STAHL: "Wild in the Streets? We've seen *Battle of Algiers.*" [*A thought balloon shows the image of a guerrilla woman, fully covered except for her eyes, planting a bomb in a cafe. The camera pans to a little boy eating ice cream.*]

What would occur in Chicago that summer, then, was a clash between *our* mythology and *their* mythology.

The *Chicago Tribune* later reported that Bob Pierson—a police provocateur disguised as a biker and acting as Jerry's bodyguard—was "in the group which lowered an American flag" in Grant Park, the incident that set off what *The Walker Report: Rights in Conflict* would officially label as "a police riot." Pierson himself wrote in *Official Detective* magazine, "I joined in the chants and taunts against the police and provoked them into hitting me with their clubs. They didn't know who I was, but they did know that I had called them names and struck them with one or more weapons."

3. "Acid Testimony"

I decide to take a tab of LSD at lunch before testifying—call me a sentimental fool—but why? Excerpt:

PAUL: "To enhance the experience. No, actually, because I wanna throw up in court. I've learned that if I drop acid with a big meal, it always makes me vomit. That way, I don't have to memorize all those dates and places. And it'll be my theatrical statement on the injustice of the trial." Abbie was furious and stopped speaking to me. Ten months later, I mailed him a movie ad—*The Professionals* was playing in our neighborhood—resulting in a reconciliation.

4. "Women's Liberation"

The purpose of this scene, taking place at the feminist protest outside the Miss America Pageant in Atlantic City, is summed up by former Yippie Robin Morgan. Excerpt:

ROBIN: "And so we say goodbye to the male-dominated peace movement. Women will no longer serve as their second-class comrades. No more working hard behind the scenes while the male superstars do all the grandstanding and get all the credit and achieve all the notoriety. No more playing a critical role in building a movement but then being denied access to the policy-making process."

(The plan was to toss tangible items of male oppression—a bridal gown, a safety razor, a girdle, high-heeled shoes, panty-hose, *Playboy* magazine, a pink brassiere—and burn them in a "Freedom Crash Can," but an ordinance forbidding *anything* to be burned on the boardwalk was enforced. Nevertheless, a burning bra has become the symbol of women's liberation. Sometimes a metaphor can serve to reveal the truth more vividly than the actual facts.)

Although Brett "loved, loved, loved" the scenes I wrote, the backers objected to the use of LSD, fearful of diverting attention from the main focus of the film. Brett's baby, diapered by the backers. I was disappointed, if only for the sake of countercultural history. The CIA originally envisioned employing LSD as a means of control; instead, for millions of young people, acid served as a vehicle to explore their own inner space, deprogramming themselves from mainstream culture and living their alternative. The CIA's scenario had backfired. Anyway, my suggestion—instead of referring to it as acid, Abbie could yell, "Hey, this is pretty powerful fuckin' aspirin"—was rejected.

Thus, the hurricane segment of the "Birth of Yippies" scene, which was originally going to open the film, has been omitted. My implied "threat" in the "Got Permit?" scene that the Yippies would pour LSD into the reservoir, plus the entire "Acid Testimony" scene, are also out. And, unfortunately, the "Women's Liberation" scene isn't included because of time restraints.

I was supposed to do the voice for my own animated character, but Abbie's son, Andrew, had auditioned to do his father's voice, and though he sounds eerily like him, he apparently wasn't a skilled actor, so it was decided to have professional actors—including Hank Azaria, Mark Ruffalo and Liev Schreiber—do *all* the voices. What a relief—I thought it was because I didn't sound enough like myself.

During an interview with Videofreex during the trial, Abbie said, "We don't wanna be martyrs. We wanna live to see the overthrow of the government. Be a great fuckin' movie." Brett's goal wasn't quite as ambitious as overthrowing the government. When he called to tell me that the documentary had been selected to open the 2007 Sundance Film Festival, he mused, "Wouldn't it be great if Abbie's legacy turns out to be that he helped to end the war in Iraq?"

I hadn't seen any of the rough cuts and didn't know what to expect at the festival screening, but Brett got a standing ovation. Although he was born two months after the protests in Chicago, he had managed—with the aid of 180 hours of film, fifty hours of video, 500 hours of audio and 23,000 pages of trial transcripts—to reveal in this neodoc the horror and the humor, the rhetoric and the reality, of those events and their aftermath, in a style and rhythm calculated to resonate with—and inspire—contemporary youth.

Yippie organizer Jim Fouratt said it "excites the imagination." Nick Nolte, who did the voice of prosecutor Thomas Foran, asked defendant Tom Hayden for his reaction. "I loved it," he replied. "I think that Brett authentically and brilliantly captured the experiences and the feelings of what we were going through." Then, turning to Brett, he added, "So thank you for the next generation from our generation."

Structurally, the film alternates between the action in the streets and the progress of the trial, with the utterly shocking imagery of defendant Bobby Seale—the national chairman of the Black Panther Party, voiced by Jeffrey Wright—being bound, gagged and shackled to his courtroom chair for insisting on his constitutional right to represent himself after being turned down by the Elmer Fudd–like Judge Julius Hoffman, voiced by the late Roy Scheider.

I would've liked to see Dick Gregory's fervent recitation of the preamble to the Declaration of Independence at an unbirthday party for LBJ, but I'm grateful for the inclusion of defendant David Dellinger saying "The power of the people is our permit" at the start of a march from the bandstand in Grant Park to the Amphitheater. And I would've liked to hear Phil Ochs's song, "I Ain't Marchin' Anymore," as the background music for that march, but I appreciate the use of Eminem's rap "Mosh" as accompaniment instead. Rather than music from the '60s, Brett preferred more contemporary groups, from Beastie Boys to Rage Against the Machine.

In fact, he had wanted to call the film *Mosh*, but *Chicago 10* encompasses the eight defendants plus attorneys William Kunstler and Leonard Weinglass. I was afraid people would think it was the ninth sequel to the musical *Chicago*. Whatever the title, athough Sundance may be a long way from Ramrod Key, the spirit of Yippie lingers on.

The defendants were found guilty, but that verdict was overturned by a judge who, ironically, had been appointed by Lyndon Johnson.

There was another screening a couple of days later, not intended so much for festivalgoers as for folks who live in Salt Lake City. I ate a chocolate candy loaded with psilocybin to enhance the experience, unaware that Brett planned to bring me onstage to speak to the audience and then join him in a Q&A session. Brett warned me, "This is the heartland." Still, I began with a joke I'd heard in town: "A Mormon decided to go hiking in the beautiful mountains of Utah, but first he stopped to buy some equipment at a mom and mom and mom and pop store." It got a really good laugh there.

One of the questions was, "What advice would you offer to young people today?" My mind was swirling like a multicolored whirlpool. I assigned my subconscious to come up with an appropriate answer, while I stalled for a moment, leaning on the lectern. "My advice to young people," I said, "is, if you go to a restaurant and order a club sandwich, be sure to remove the toothpick before you take the first bite." When my subconscious came through, I said, "Always remember that the political system acts as a buffer between the status quo and the force of evolution. Example: In order to get Republican votes for the children's health care bill, Democrats agreed to fund $28 million to their abstinence-only program."

Brett wanted *Chicago 10* to open during the election year, so he was pleased that it opened in theaters around the country in February 2008 and was on PBS two weeks before the election. In October 2007, *Chicago 10* opened the Austin Film Festival. Brett was unable to attend, so I went there as his proxy. In the morning, I was interviewed on radio station KLBJ. Cartoonist Ethan Persoff (who, incidentally, has been putting up a Web site, "The Realist Archive Project," posting four issues at a time) had moved to Austin ten years earlier and recalls:

"The metal band Nashville Pussy was being interviewed. The DJ said, 'Next up it's Nashville P—well, what can we say? It's a word we can't say on air that's a synonym for kitten. Welcome to KLBJ.' Right off the bat, a member of the band asks, 'KLBJ—Isn't El B.J. Spanish for blow job?' They must have had the delay button right in the radio booth, because you could hear someone slap something but miss, knocking over a coffee cup or bumping into a microphone. It all got on the air. The DJ cut to a station break too late. Actually, LBJ stands for Lyndon [Baines] Johnson. KLBJ is owned and controlled by the Johnson family."

I decided to smoke a joint before I left my hotel for the screening that evening. However, I was in a nonsmoking room, and there was a notice on the desk: "Should you choose to smoke in a nonsmoking room, a $250 cleaning/deodorizing surcharge will be added to your room bill." So I toked it in the bathroom with the door closed, sitting on the tub and exhaling into the toilet.

During the Q&A session, someone asked if we hadn't provoked the police. Others in the audience berated him.

"Wait," I said, "let him talk. It's a fair question." Focusing on the individual who asked it, I added, "Don't worry, I won't let anybody Taser you." (This was a reference to the incident in September at the University of Florida, where, during a Q&A with the speaker, Senator John Kerry, a student peppered him with questions—about impeaching George Bush, why he didn't challenge the 2004 election results, and whether both he and Bush were in the secret Skull and Bones society as undergraduates at Yale—and refused repeated requests by other students to leave the microphone after his allotted time was up. University police tried to remove him from the auditorium, and when he resisted, they Tasered him.) "Yes," I answered, "the Chicago police were provoked—by police provocateurs. . . . "

Another question dealt with the comparisons and contrasts between the wars in Vietnam and Iraq, and what was necessary to challenge the latter.

"Imagination," I replied. "Both wars were both based on lies and fear-mongering. They both resorted to euphemisms as a form of disinformation. In Southeast Asia, concentration camps were called strategic hamlets. In the so-called war on terror, torture is referred to as enhanced interrogation techniques. . . . One of the differences is that there was a draft during the Vietnam War. That personalized it, sadly. People wore buttons that said, 'Not With My Body You Don't.' The Bush administration deliberately doesn't have a draft now, because they know that whatever disconnect there is between the public and the horror that the government is conducting in their name, would dissolve. People would take to the streets in multitudes to demonstrate against the war. When Latinos marched through Los Angeles over the immigration issue, there were a million of them. What we need to do now is hire Mexican workers as guest protesters, so they can do the job that Americans don't want to do. . . ."

At one point during the Q&A, I surrendered to an impulse. Pretending that my cell phone was vibrating, I took it out of my pocket and said hello, then told the audience, "It's Rudy Giuliani's wife."

While Giuliani was speaking before the National Rifle Association earlier that month, his cell phone had rung. "Let's see now," he said to the audience. "This is my wife calling." He pressed the Talk button. "Hello, dear. I'm talking to the members of the NRA right now. Would you like to say hello? . . . I love you, and I'll give you a call as soon as I'm finished, okay? . . . Okay, have a safe trip. Bye-bye. Talk to you later, dear. I love you." It seemed like a totally contrived gimmick, a blatant attempt to humanize himself, sucking up to the Republican base by emphasizing family values in the face of two failed marriages and being hated by his own offspring.

The *Wall Street Journal* estimated that, prior to this

staged stunt at the NRA, it could have happened "more than forty times." Giuliani explained that, since 9/11, he and his wife made a habit of calling each other whenever they get on a plane in order to "reaffirm the fact that we love each other." He admits, "I've been married three times. I can't afford to lose another one. I'm sure you understand." When his cell-phone ploy occurred while speaking to a group of Cuban Americans in Florida, he said, "I just wanted to see that she was doing okay," adding that his wife was learning Spanish.

In Austin, I noticed that another animated reenactment scene was missing. Abbie Hoffman got arrested in Chicago for having the word FUCK printed on his forehead with lipstick, an idea borrowed from Lenny Bruce, who, I told Abbie, had once printed FUCK on *his* forehead with strips of wet paper towel from a courthouse bathroom, in order to discourage photographers from taking his picture. Abbie might have gotten away with it if only he hadn't tipped his hat to the police who were sitting in their car in front of the house where we were staying, waiting for us to start the day. They followed us to a restaurant, where they asked Abbie to take off his hat, and when he did, they told him he was under arrest.

"It's the duty of a revolutionist to finish breakfast," he replied, but the cops disagreed with his premise. They handcuffed him and proceeded to drag him out of the restaurant, forcing me to eat the rest of his breakfast.

THE GRATEFUL DEAD PLAY THE PYRAMIDS

September 2008 marked the thirtieth anniversary of the Grateful Dead's unforgettable concerts in Egypt. Although

Rhino Records released a double-CD album with a DVD of the event, I was fortunate enough to be there with Ken Kesey and a bunch of Merry Pranksters. The Dead were scheduled to perform on three successive nights at an open-air theater in front of the Pyramids, with the Sphinx keeping close watch.

Bob Weir looked up at the Great Pyramid and cried out, "What *is* it!" Actually, it was the place for locals to go on a cheap date. The Pyramids were surrounded by moats of discarded bottle caps. A bootleg tape of Dean Martin and Jerry Lewis doing filthy schtick was being used for a preliminary sound check. Later, an American general complained to stage manager Steve Parish that the decadence of a rock 'n' roll band performing here was a sacrilege to 5,000 years of history.

"Listen," Parish said, "I lost two brothers in 'Nam, and I don't wanna hear this crap."

The general retreated in the face of those imaginary brothers. There were a couple of *real* injured veterans, though. Drummer Bill Kreutzmann had fallen off a horse and broken his arm, but he would still be playing with the band, using *one* drumstick. And faithful Deadhead Bill Walton's buttocks had been used as a pincushion by the Portland Traiblazers' doctor so that he could continue to play basketball even though the bones of his foot were being shattered with pain he coudn't feel. Having been injected with painkilling drugs to hide the greed rather than heal the injury, he had to walk around with crutches. Maybe Kreutzmann and Walton could team up and enter the half-upside-down sack race.

An air of incredible excitement permeated the first night. Never had the Dead been so inspired. Backstage,

Jerry Garcia was giving final instructions to the band: "Remember, play in tune." The music began with Egyptian oudist Hamza El Din, backed up by a group tapping out ancient rhythms on their 14-inch-diameter tars—pizza-like drums—soon joined by drummer Mickey Hart, Garcia ambled on with a gentle guitar riff, then Kreutzmann, Phil Lesh, Donna, Keith, and as the Dead meshed with the local percussion ensemble, basking in total respect of each other, Weir segued into the forceful opening chords of Buddy Holly's "Not Fade Away."

"Did you see that?" Kesey shouted. "The Sphinx's jaw just dropped!"

Every morning, my Prankster roommate, George Walker, got up early and climbed to the top of the Pyramid. He was in training. It was to be his honor to plant a Grateful Dead flag on top of the Great Pyramid. He would attach it to a pole at the peak of the pyramid where the stone block that should've been the final piece was missing.

Pranksters Mountain Girl Goldie Rush and I decided to score some hashish at a courtyard in the oldest section of Cairo. It came in long thick slabs, and we eagerly sat down on benches to sample it. The official task of a teenage boy was to light the "hubbly-bubbly," a giant water pipe that used hot coals to keep the hash burning and us sweating like crazy.

Later, I found myself sitting and chanting in a tublike sarcophagus (burial tomb) with fantastic acoustics, at the center of gravity in the Great Pyramid, after having ingested liquid LSD that a Prankster had smuggled into Egypt in a plastic Visine bottle. It was only as I breathed in deeply before each extended *Om* that I was forced to ponder the mystery of those who urinate there.

There was something especially magical about the third concert on Saturday. I had a strong feeling that I was involved in a *lesson*. It was as though the secret of the Dead would finally be revealed to me, if only I paid proper attention. That night would feature a full eclipse of the moon, and Egyptian kids were running through the streets shaking tin cans filled with rocks in order to bring it back.

"It's okay," I assured them, "the Grateful Dead will bring back the moon."

And, sure enough, a rousing rendition of "Ramble On Rose" would accomplish that feat. The moon returned just as the marijuana cookie that rock impresario Bill Graham gave me started blending in with the other drugs. Graham no longer wore two wristwatches, one for each coast. He now wore one wristwatch with two faces. There was a slight problem with an amplifier, but a sound engineer said that it was "getting there."

"Getting there ain't good enough," Garcia replied. "It's gotta fuckin' *be* there."

This was a totally outrageous event. The line between incongruity and appropriateness had disappeared along with the moon. The music was so powerful that the only way to go was ecstatic. That night, when the Dead played "Fire on the Mountain," I danced my ass off with all the others on that outdoor stage as if I had no choice.

"You know," Bill Graham confessed, "this is the first time I ever danced in public."

"Me too," I said.

That was the lesson.

4.

SEVERAL DEAD ICONS

GINSBERG'S LAST LAUGH

Our paths had often crossed—at civil rights marches, antiwar rallies, marijuana smoke-ins, environmental demonstrations—he was always on the front lines, especially when it came to gay rights. Long before Ellen DeGeneres came out on a sitcom, Allen Ginsberg came out in the streets. On those occasions when we both performed at a benefit, I could hear his laughter reverberating from backstage like a Tibetan gong.

In the summer of 1982, there was a celebration of the twenty-fifth anniversary of Jack Kerouac's *On the Road* at Naropa, a Buddhist college in Boulder, Colorado, where presumably they refer to his book as *On the Path*. I was invited to moderate a discussion, "Political Fallout of the Beat Generation." The panelists: Ginsberg, William Burroughs, Abbie Hoffman and Timothy Leary. We were all asked to sign posters for the event. Hoffman wrote his signature extra large, with great care.

He explained, "The guy who shot John Lennon complained that Lennon gave him a sloppy autograph, so I ain't takin' any chances."

During the panel, Ginsberg said, "I think there was one slight shade of error in describing the Beat movement as primarily a protest movement. That was the thing that Kerouac was always complaining about. He felt the literary aspect or the spiritual aspect or the emotional aspect was not so much protest at all, but a declaration of unconditioned mind beyond protest, beyond resentment, beyond loser, beyond *winner*—*way* beyond winner—beyond winner or loser . . . but the basic thing that I understood and dug Jack for was unconditioned mind, negative capability, totally open mind—beyond victory or defeat. Just awareness, and that was the humor, and that's what the saving grace is. That's why there *will* be political aftereffects, but it doesn't have to win because having to win a revolution is like having to make a milliion dollars."

As moderator, I asked, "Abbie, since you used to quote Che Guevara saying, 'In a revolution, one wins or dies,' do you have a response to that?"

HOFFMAN: "All right, Ginzo. Poems have a lot of different meanings for different people. For me, your poem *Howl* was a call to arms."

GINSBERG: "A whole boatload of sentimental bullshit."

HOFFMAN: "We saw in the sixties a great imbalance of power, and the only way that you could correct that imbalance was to organize people and to fight for power. Power is not a dirty word. The concept of trying to win against social injustice is not a dirty kind of concept. It all depends on how you define the game, how you define winning and how you define losing—that's the Zen trip that was learned by defining that you were the prophets and we were the warriors. I'm saying that you didn't fight, but you were the fighters. And I'll tell you, If you don't think you were a political movement and you don't like winning, the fuckin' lawyer that defended *Howl* in some goddamn obscenity suit—you wanted *him* to be a fuckin' winner, I guarantee you that. That *was* a political debate. . . ."

Ironically, Ginsberg was very insecure about *Howl*, and he questioned the big fuss over it. "There shouldn't be a trial over *this* poem," he once lamented. In fact, a biography of Ginsberg—*American Scream* by Jonah Raskin—has a surprising revelation: "In the mid-1970s, in the midst of the counterculture he had helped to create, he promised to rewrite *Howl*. Now that he was a hippie minstrel and a Pied Piper for the generation that advocated peace and love, he would alter *Howl*, he said, so that it might reflect the euphoria of the hippies. He would include a 'positive redemptive catalogue,' he said."

The much-repeated opening line of *Howl* was, "I saw the best minds of my generation destroyed by madness, starving hysterical naked. . . ." Hoffman sure would've been shocked to learn that Ginsberg had planned to rewrite *Howl*, this time beginning with an upbeat line: "I saw the best minds of my generation turned on by music."

Indeed, Ginsberg sought out musicians—the Beatles, Bob Dylan, the Clash, Jello Biafra, Beck—exulting in their talent and status, and wrestling with his own ego in the process. In fact, a few days before his death, Ginsberg wrote to Bill Clinton, revealing that his days were numbered, and asking the president, "If you have some sort of reward or medal for service in art or poetry, please send one along."

Ginsberg once asked his father if life was worth living. His father answered, "It depends on the liver." This was a touch of inadvertent prophecy; Allen died of liver cancer on April 5, 1997. He had lived his life to the hilt and beyond, balancing with dignity and grace on the cusp of rationalism and mysticism, one individual, with curiosity and compassion for all. On April 7, Michael Krasny hosted a memorial for Ginsberg on his radio program, *Forum*, over KQED-FM in San Francisco. The panel included novelist/Prankster Ken Kesey, poet/publisher Lawrence Ferlinghetti, Digger/actor Peter Coyote and me. The following is excerpted from that conference call.

KESEY: "I was at a party one time, when I first knew Ginsberg, and he was standing by himself over by the fireplace, with a wine glass in his hand, and people milling around, and finally some young girl sort of broke off from the rest of the crowd and approached him and said, 'I can't talk to you—you're a legend.' And he said, 'Yes, but I'm a friendly legend.'"

FERLINGHETTI: "He lived so many flames. Today the youth, like the 20-year-olds, are really turned on to Ginsberg and the Beat poets, but the thing they're turned on to is the apolitical part. One forgets how political the Beats were in the '50s, which was the Eisenhower and McCarthy era. And that's a flame that seems to be flickering these days."

KESEY: "He was a great warrior. I think that's more important than his poetry. In fact, in later times, I haven't read much of his poetry at all, because the warrior aspect of Ginsberg has loomed much larger. When we went to the Vietnam Day parade up in Berkeley, they had been interviewing the Hells Angels—all the Hells Angels were gonna come out and oppose the opposers—they were gonna come out and start a riot, is what it was.

"So Allen asked me to take him up there, to where the Angels hung out in this big white house in Oakland, and we went in there, and here's all these big brutes holding their beer cans, with their beer bellies and their beards, and Ginsberg goes right in and starts talking to them. And you look around, here are these great big mean-looking guys wearing swastikas, pretty soon Ginsberg has just charmed the hell out of 'em, until there's *not* gonna be a riot. He took himself into that—they marveled at him. It was the courage, again, the courage of this man to come into this situation and defuse it."

KRASSNER: "I knew Allen more as a researcher and an activist than as a poet. Abbie Hoffman and other political activists like Ed Sanders were influenced by *Howl*, but as a researcher, Ginsberg had meticulously acquired files on everything that the CIA ever did, and I'm happy that these are included in his archives [at Stanford University].

"The one image I have of him from Chicago in 1968, when we were holding our Yippie counter-convention—as opposed to the Democratic 'convention of death,' as we called it—the police were in Lincoln Park tear-gassing and clubbing people, and Ginsberg sat in the middle of it like some kind of stoned Buddha, chanting *Om* over and over again, and people gathered around him, and he led them out of the park, and it created a kind of mystical force field, so that the cops just ignored them, and he was like the Pied Piper of Peacemaking. Allen just articulated the consciousness of people who knew that the mainstream culture was a sadomasochistic bizarre mess."

KRASNY: "What do you do with the kind of bizarre mess

that some people would claim is characteristic of Ginsberg in the wake of his death, all the NAMBLA [North American Man/Boy Love Association] stuff, and his apparently not only supporting that organization, but also expressing favor where little boys are concerned, sexually, and also using drugs somewhat recklessly and excessively as some attribute to him?"

KRASSNER: "Well, that's the risk of free will. Allen has always admitted, you know, he would go to a poetry reading and say he was hoping to meet a young boy there. He was honest about his perversion of pedophilia, if that's what it was, but it may have been just a fantasy. He was for dialogue, and he was nonviolent, so it's just interesting as to what he considered the age of consent. A few months ago he told me it was 18."

COYOTE: [*chuckling*] "It's just so funny. I mean, as a father of two kids, I'm *repulsed* by the idea of pedophilia, but you know, by the same token, it's Allen. It probably wasn't easy being Allen. It's easier to be some of us than others of us, and I think that Allen's great courage was to be unequivocally who he was. And when he went to Cuba and announced that he wanted to have oral sex with Che Guevara, it actually was to Castro's detriment, in my mind, that he threatened to lock him up, or threw him out.

"The thing that Allen represented to me was more than the Beats, more than anything else—I harken back to Gary Snyder's great phrase, "the great underground," which he calls the tradition, coming from the Paleolithic shamans on up to the present—the tradition of yogins and healers and midwives and poets and artists and people who stand for archaic, earth-centered values, life-supporting values. It's like a great river that kind of surfaces in various cultures around the world at different times. It's squench-less, transcendentalist for just one little rivulet of it. And Allen was a great prophet for it."

KESEY: "When we [Merry Pranksters] went to see Leary at Millbrook, Ginsberg was on the bus, and we had pulled over somewhere, and he was up immediately, sweeping the stuff out of the bus with a little broom, and Cassady at the wheel said, 'Looky there, it's our Jewish mother.' And he *was* the Jewish mother, in some way, to a whole literary movement. He did all he could to help all of his friends get into print, all the time. He was a great benefactor to this art, and worked very, very hard to have his friends have as much fame as he did.

"We had a poetry festival some years ago up here in Oregon, and the way we were doing it, during the day we had a stage outside of our basketball court, and we had headliners that were gonna be on that night, and during the day people read poetry and we judged it, and they were gonna be the people that read with Ginsberg, and during the day all the people in the field outside gradually trickled into the basketball court, like 3,000 people in there, and we were gonna charge them $5 apiece, but they were already in there. Allen said, 'Let me see what I can do.' And he got up there with his harmonium, and he began, *Om, Om.* Pretty soon he had 'em all *Om Om*ing, and he just gave a gesture like that, stood up, walked out, and 3,000 people walked out with him, so we were able to charge 'em money."

KRASSNER: "We've been praising Allen so much, but I'll give you one little revealing story. On one hand, he was a pacifist. I remember when he first started taking LSD, and he thought that world peace would come about if only

John F. Kennedy and Nikita Khrushchev would take acid together. And yet, I remember a scene—this was in the early '70s—Ken Kesey and I and my daughter Holly, who was a young girl then, were visiting William Burroughs in New York, and he had this huge loft, and a cat, and a lot of cardboard boxes, and he was wearing a suit and tie and high-top red sneakers.

"We all decided to visit Ginsberg in the hospital—he'd had a stroke, and part of his face was paralyzed—he was in bed there, and I introduced him to my daughter, and he graciously struggled to sit up and shake hands with her. But he was kind of weak and deep into some kind of medication, and he blurted out—what they would call in psychiatry a "primary process"—he blurted out, 'Henry Kissinger should have his head chopped off!' It was some kind of Ginsbergian Tourette's syndrome."

KRASNY: "There's been a lot of solemn talk, so I'm glad you added that note of levity. Ginsberg would want, I think, a discussion about his life to be infused with a lot of humor and satire, don't you think?"

KRASSNER: "Oh, absolutely. You can't take yourself too seriously if you're walking around with an Uncle Sam hat and Mahatma Gandhi pajamas, chanting 'The war is over' when the war was at its height. But that act inspired Phil Ochs to write his song 'The War Is Over' and to organize rallies in Los Angeles and New York on the theme of 'The war is over.'"

COYOTE: "I think that Ginsberg represented an enlarged notion of sanity—which is not to say it's not without contradictions, which is not to say it's not as stained and tattered as anything else. You may not like the fact that Gandhi tested his celibacy by lying naked with young girls, or that Freud was shooting cocaine while he was working out his psychotherapy theories, or that Martin Luther King had sex with women outside of marriage, but to me, what these facts do is reinforce the humanity of the person in question and remind us that we don't have to be perfect to make contributions, that we can struggle against the dark or the undeveloped sides of our nature and still make a contribution, and I think that's kind of the beacon Allen is. The thrust and underpinnings of his life were fundamentally sane in every venue. That's really what I respect him most for."

FERLINGHETTI: "I think maybe you could say Allen started out mad and became *saner* all his life, and then he became more quiet, I think, in his last years, and this was an influence of Buddhism, I believe. He died as a Buddhist, he didn't want any support systems. There were Buddhists around him at all-night vigils the last two nights, and he died the way he wanted to die."

KESEY: "Ginsberg had a terrific laugh. I was just trying to think, what was I going to miss most? Even in the most serious moments, this thing would bubble up and bark forth, his eyes twinkling. It was a great laugh, and I'm gonna miss him."

ROBERT ANTON WILSON: "KEEP THE LASAGNA FLYING"

Most likely your daily newspaper didn't acknowledge the death of Robert Anton Wilson on January 11, 2007. He was 74. The prolific author and countercultural icon had been suffering from post-polio syndrome. Caregivers read all of his late wife Arlen's poetry to him at his bedside and e-mailed me: "He was quite cheered up by the time we left.

He definitely needed to die. His body was turning on him in ways that would not allow him to rest."

In his final blog five days earlier, Wilson wrote: "I don't see how to take death seriously. I look forward without dogmatic optimism, but without dread. I love you all and I deeply implore you to keep the lasagna flying." Actually, it was expected that he would die seven months earlier. On June 19, 2006, he sent this haiku (with one syllable missing) to his electronic cabal:

> Well what do you know?
> Another day has passed
> and I'm still not not.

We originally became friends in 1959 when his first published article graced the cover of *The Realist*. It was titled "The Semantics of God," and he suggested that "The Believer had better face himself and ask squarely: Do I literally believe that 'God' has a penis? If the answer is no, then it seems only logical to drop the ridiculous practice of referring to 'God' as 'he.'" Wilson then began writing a regular column, "Negative Thinking."

In 1964, I ran another front-cover story by him, "Timothy Leary and His Psychological H-Bomb," which began: "The future may decide that the two greatest thinkers of the 20th Century were Albert Einstein, who showed how to create atomic fission in the physical world, and Timothy Leary, who showed how to create atomic fission in the psychological world. The latter discovery may be more important than the former; there are some reasons for thinking that it was made necessary by the former. Leary may have shown how our habits of thought can be changed."

Wilson took that notion as his personal marching orders, altering the consciousness of countless grateful readers of his thirty-five books—from *Sex, Drugs & Magick* to *Everything Is Under Control: An Encyclopedia of Conspiracy Theories*—all written with the aid of that good old creative fuel, marijuana. He once told me about his creative process: "It's rather obsessive-compulsive, I think. I write the first draft straight, then rewrite stoned, then rewrite straight again, then rewrite stoned again, and so on, until I'm absolutely delighted with every sentence, or irate editors start reminding me about deadlines—whichever comes first."

He became a pothead in 1955, but a few years ago he told the audience at a Prophets Conference, "I haven't smoked pot in about twelve . . . hours, and I want you to know it's great to be clean." He enjoyed peppering his presentations at such distinguished New Age events with "motherfuckers" and "cocksuckers," and was disinvited from participating in future Prophet Conferences because, said the organizers, "What we feel to be important to your insights are being lost to the audience when packaged in hard and harsh language."

Wilson once described his writings as "intellectual comedy." He told an Internet database, *Contemporary Authors*: "If my books do what I intend, they should leave the reader feeling that the universe is capable of doing something totally shocking and unexpected in the next five minutes. I am trying to show that life without certainty can be exhilarating, liberating, a great adventure." He called his philosophy "Maybe Logic," which became the title of a documentary about him.

Stephen Gaskin, founder of The Farm commune, writes, "I had the good fortune to visit with Robert at his house and meet his wife. When I saw the beautiful relationship between them, I understood why the sex scenes in his books are so nicely written that they stand out above everyone else's sex scenes that I've read. One of my next encounters with him was standing on the sidewalk of a cold November day in Amsterdam waiting for a taxi. He didn't have enough of a coat, and he was standing in the cold with his collar turned up and his hands stuck in his pockets. It was a while after his wife had died and he looked quite forlorn. We collected him up, put a warm coat on him, and put a joint in his mouth. It was a real hoot to get to be friends with one of my very favorite writers. His book *The Illuminatus* is a benchmark in science fiction and contemporary paranoia."

Wilson wrote his own obituary in an autobiography, *Cosmic Trigger*: "According to reliable sources, I died on February 22, 1994—George Washington's birthday. I felt nothing special or shocking at the time, and believed that I still sat at my word processor working on a novel called *Bride of Illuminatus*. At lunch-time, however, when I checked my voice mail, I found that Tim Leary and a dozen friends had already called to ask to speak to me, or— if they still believed in Reliable Sources—to offer support and condolences to my grieving family. I quickly gathered that the news of my tragic end had appeared on the Internet: 'Noted science-fiction author Robert Anton Wilson was found dead in his home yesterday, apparently the victim of a heart attack. [He] was noted for his libertarian viewpoints, love of technology and off the wall humor. Mr. Wilson is survived by his wife and two children.'"

R.U. Sirius, co-author of *Counterculture Through the Ages*, writes, "Robert Anton Wilson enjoyed his first death so much, he decided to try it again. As the result of medical expenses and problems with the IRS, he found himself in a financial squeeze towards the end of his life. Word went out and the Internet community responded by sending him $68,000 within the first couple of days. This allowed him to die with the comfort, grace and dignity that he deserved. He taught us all that 'the universe contains a maybe.' So maybe there is an afterlife, and maybe Bob's consciousness is hovering around all of us who were touched by his words and his presence all these years. And if that's the case, I'm sure he'd like to see you do something strange and irreverent—and yet beautiful—in his honor."

WHO THE HELL IS STEW ALBERT?

After Larry "Ratso" Sloman ghost-wrote Howard Stern's autobiography, *Private Parts*, he compiled an oral biography of Abbie Hoffman, *Steal This Dream*. Stern wasn't impressed.

"Well," said Ratso, "Stew Albert likes it."

"Who the hell is Stew Albert?"

Stew was the first one to turn me on with marijuana. We met in 1965 when I was invited to emcee the first Vietnam teach-in on the UC Berkeley campus, and he introduced me to a supersize Thai stick. "Now I know why we're fighting in Southeast Asia," I observed—"to protect the crops." That quote became a headline on the front page of the *Berkeley Barb*, together with a photo of me smoking a joint.

Stew never got the media attention that Abbie Hoffman and Jerry Rubin did as co-organizers of the Yippies, although he was the personification of an activist.

He also served as a behind-the-scenes peacemaker. During the protests in 1968 at the Democrats' convention in Chicago, Abbie bought a pig to run as the Yippie candidate for president, but Jerry thought it wasn't big enough or ugly enough, so Stew went with him to buy another pig, bigger and uglier.

Stew was the first demonstrator there to get hit by the police with a billy club. After his head was stitched and bandaged, we went to a Western Union office and sent a telegram (recently deemed an obsolescent means of communication) to the United Nations, requesting them to send in a human rights unit to investigate violations in Chicago. Stew, who had acted as a liaison between the Yippies and the Black Panther Party, told me, "Malcolm X, and then the Black Panthers, had planned to take their case to the UN."

We were both unindicted co-conspirators for crossing state lines to foment rioting, unindicted because they were afraid we would have a freedom-of-the-press defense. In addition to our being there as protesters, Stew covered the counter-convention for the *Berkeley Barb*, and I covered it for *The Realist*.

I published a couple of Stew's articles, one on the legacy of Che Guevara, another on Stew's campaign for sheriff in Alameda County. He came in fourth, winning in Berkeley with 65,000 votes. Later, he became a go-between for Timothy Leary and Eldridge Cleaver in Algeria. Leary wanted to take LSD with Cleaver, who told Stew that he was afraid Leary would try to program him, but Cleaver said yes to acid, provided he could wear his gun during the trip.

Stew died at the age of 66. I'll miss his integrity, his

passion and his sense of humor. When he wrote a memoir, he decided to title it *Who the Hell Is Stew Albert?*

Previously, he had co-edited with his wife, Judy Gumbo, *The Sixties Papers*, a collection of documents underlying the countercultural history of that era, from Tom Hayden's "Port Huron Statement"—the credo of SDS (Students For a Democratic Society), currently undergoing a rebirth on campuses—to Robin Morgan's feminist manifesto, "Goodbye to All That."

Albert and Gumbo had found an illegal surveillance device under their car; they sued the FBI and won. Ironically, part of the settlement enabled them to buy a computer, with which they produced that book, now used in college courses across the country.

KURT VONNEGUT LIVES!

Several months before Timothy Leary died, he told me, "I watch words now. It's an obsession. I learned it from Marshall McLuhan, of course. A terrible vice. Had it for years, but not actually telling people about it. I watch the words that people use. The medium is the message, you recall. The brain creates the realities she wants. When we see the prisms that these words come through, we can understand."

During the Cold War, hysteria over the word "Communist" was the forerunner of current hysteria over the word "terrorist." The attorney general of Arizona rejected the Communist Party's request for a place on the ballot because state law "prohibits official representation" for the Communists, and in addition, "The subversive nature of your organization is even more clearly designated by the fact that you do not even include your zip code." Alvin Dark, manager of the Giants, announced, "Any pitcher who throws at a batter and deliberately tries to hit him is a Communist." And singer Pat Boone declared at the Greater New York Anti-Communism Rally in Madison Square Garden, "I would rather see my four daughters shot before my eyes than have them grow up in a Communist United States. I would rather see those kids blown into Heaven than taught into Hell by the Communists."

In a foreword to a collection of my satire, *The Winner of the Slow Bicycle Race*, Kurt Vonnegut wrote: "Paul Krassner in 1963 created a miracle of compressed intelligence nearly as admirable for potent simplicity, in my opinion, as Einstein's e=mc^2. With the Vietnam War going on, and its critics discounted and scorned by the government and the mass media, Krassner put on sale a red, white and blue poster that said FUCK COMMUNISM.

"At the beginning of the 1960s, FUCK was believed to be so full of bad magic as to be unprintable. In the most humanely influential American novel of this half-century, *The Catcher in the Rye*, Holden Caulfield, it will be remembered, was shocked to see that word on a sub-way-station wall. He wondered what seeing it might do to the mind of a little kid. COMMUNISM was to millions the name of the most loathsome evil imaginable. To call an American a communist was like calling somebody a Jew in Nazi Germany. By having FUCK and COMMU-NISM fight it out in a single sentence, Krassner wasn't merely being funny as heck. He was demonstrating how preposterous it was for so many people to be responding to both words with such cockamamie Pavlovian fear and alarm."

On the evening of March 14, 2007, at about 8:15 p.m., Vonnegut was sitting on the stoop in front of his house—smoking a cigarette, of course. When he stood up, he lost his balance and fell. Although he was supposedly brain dead at the precise moment his head hit the steps, he was kept on life support for the next few weeks. When it became clear that he could never be revived, the decision was made to remove life support, as he had requested.

The news of his actual death on April 11, our mutual friend Robert Weide (who directed the film version of Vonnegut's novel *Mother Night*) told me, "was merely a postscript—a relief, actually—which is not to say it was so easy to process. I'd equate it to losing a family member, albeit one who had a long, incredible life—one who changed the lives and worldview of countless people who had never met him, and who remained entirely lucid and kept his miraculous sense of humor to the very end."

The obituaries all seemed to stress how depressed Vonnegut was, never failing to mention his failed attempt at committing suicide. So naturally I had been pleasantly surprised when this professional pessimist told me that my satire made him feel *hopeful*.

"You made supposedly serious matters seem ridiculous," he explained, "and this inspired many of your readers to decide for themselves what was ridiculous and what was not. Knowing that people were doing that, better late than never, made me optimistic."

Nonetheless, he once summed up his concern over the environment in a bumper sticker he sent me: "Your Planet's Immune System Is Trying to Get Rid of You."

A couple of years before George Bush finally admitted in his State of the Union address that the United States is addicted to oil, Vonnegut stated, "Our government is conducting a war against drugs, is it? Let them go after petroleum. Talk about a destructive high! You put some of this stuff in your car and you can go a hundred miles an hour, run over the neighbor's dog and tear the atmosphere to smithereens."

In his book *A Man Without a Country*, he continued on with that conundrum: "Our government's got a war on drugs. That's certainly a lot better than no drugs at all. That's what was said about prohibition. Do you realize that from 1919 to 1933 it was absolutely against the law to manufacture, transport or sell alcoholic beverages, and an Indiana newspaper humorist said, 'Prohibition is better than no liquor at all.'"

Vonnegut himself was a mass of contradictions.

He was a Luddite who hated newfangled contraptions—though he often used a fax, he refused to use e-mail—he also said, "I think that novels that leave out technology misrepresent life as badly as Victorians misrepresented life by leaving out sex." He advised young would-be writers to "never use semi-colons—all they do is suggest you've been to college," but he also wrote, "When Ernest Hemingway killed himself he put a period at the end of his life; old age is more like a semi-colon." He was the honorary president of the American Humanist Association—"We humanists try to behave as decently, as fairly and as honorably as we can without any expectation of rewards or punishments in an afterlife"—but he also wanted his epitaph to read, "The Only Proof He Needed for the Existence of God Was Music."

Vonnegut was really a closet optimist. That's revealed by his response to a fan who had sent him a letter in which she wrote, "I'd love to know your thoughts for a woman of 43 who is finally going to have a child but is wary of bringing a new life into such a frightening world."

Vonnegut wanted to tell her, "Don't do it! It could be another George Bush. The kid would be lucky to be born into a society where even the poor people are overweight but unlucky to be in one without a national health plan or decent public education for most, where lethal injection and warfare are forms of entertainment, so either go on practicing safe sex or emigrate."

Instead, he replied, "What made being alive almost worthwhile for me was all the saints I've met, who could be anywhere." He explained that, "By saints, I meant people who behaved decently in a strikingly indecent society."

The first time I met Vonnegut was at a memorial for Abbie Hoffman, whom he referred to as "the holy antiwar clown." The last time I saw him was at a panel on humor and satire at the Ethical Culture Society of New York. The panelists were Vonnegut, the late columnist Art Buchwald, stand-up comic Barry Crimmins and myself. All four of us had written books published by Seven Stories Press, but when the panel concluded, the longest line waiting to have those books signed was overwhelmingly for Vonnegut.

He loved to make people laugh at his own despair over the way the American Dream has morphed into an American nightmare. During the panel, he talked about the hellishness of living on earth. So, later that evening, Nancy handed him a parody of a Monopoly card showing the rich-guy logo jumping away from flames, with this caption: "Get Out of Hell Free."

A year and a half later, Vonnegut finally accomplished that goal.

"Life," he once wrote, "is my avocation. Death is my vocation."

PETER STAFFORD MEETS TOM SNYDER

A couple of old acquaintances died recently.

One was Peter Stafford, co-author of the classic *Psychedelics Encyclopedia*. In an early issue of *High Times*, he co-authored an article titled "Who Turned On Whom." That's the way LSD use got spread around, by word of mouth. Timothy Leary once told me about the use of LSD by Herman Kahn, director of the Hudson Institute, a conservative think tank, and author of *On Thermonuclear War*. I argued that despite taking acid, Kahn still continued his game of war planning for the Pentagon.

"Herman is often misunderstood," Leary replied. "He is not a war planner, he's a civil defense planner. Herman's claim is that he is one of the few highly placed Americans who's willing to gaze with naked eyes upon the possibilities of atomic warfare and come up with solutions to this horrible possibility. Perhaps his LSD sessions have given him this revelation and courage. And even his phrase 'spasm war,' which to the intellectual liberal sounds gruesome, is a powerful, cellular metaphor describing an event which the very phrase itself, 'spasm war,' might prevent."

Herman Kahn had a request. He wanted me to guide him on a tour of the Lower East Side. When we met, his assistant, Anthony Wiener, was there. (He was the conduit for CIA funding of the MK-ULTRA project, which used LSD in behavior-modification experiments with unaware subjects.) Wiener was recommending a film, *The War Game*, to Kahn.

"How does it scan?" asked Kahn.

"It scans beautiful. But you really ought to see it, Herman. You're in it."

"Why? I saw *Dr. Strangelove*. I was in that."

Wiener went on his way, and I led Kahn to the Underground Head Shop, where he bought a poster that warned, "Chicken Little Was Right!" Then I brought him to Tompkins Square Park and told him about the police attack on hippies there. Kahn's point of view was that of one who attempts to create an objective scenario by extrapolating from the past and present as the basis for his predictions of the future.

"The hippie dropout syndrome is delaying the guaranteed annual wage," he said.

I told him that the CIA was running opium dens around Cambodia. He wasn't surprised, he said, because they smoke dope and show affection with equal openness. Kahn was present when a Laotian general was briefing John Kennedy in the White House.

"The trouble with your people," the exasperated president complained, "is that they'd rather fuck than fight."

"Wouldn't you?" the general responded.

Kahn and I stopped at a bookstore on St. Marks Place.

"I'll show you the books I bought," I said, "if you'll show me the books you bought."

"You know," he confessed, "when I was three years old, I said to a little girl, 'I'll show you mine if you'll show me yours'—and she wouldn't do it—now you'll print that because I was frustrated as a child, I want to blow up the world."

Among the books he purchased was *LSD—The*

Problem-Solving Psychedelic, co-authored by Peter Stafford. That's Peter's legacy—he was so far ahead of the curve he served as a guide for a professional think-tanker.

◆ ◆ ◆

The other death was TV personality Tom Snyder. On his late-night show, *Tomorrow*, his guests ranged from Jimmy Hoffa to John Lennon, from Ayn Rand to Muhammad Ali, from Charles Manson to Jerry Garcia. For the first ten minutes of his interview with musician Meat Loaf, he kept calling him Meatball. In 1978, when I was a guest on his show in Los Angeles, I ingested magic mushrooms in order to enhance the experience.

I lived in San Francisco, where an ex-cop had just assassinated Mayor George Moscone and Supervisor Harvey Milk, only a week after the poisoned Kool-Aid massacre in Jonestown by San Francisco cult leader Jim Jones. Snyder mentioned it, and I brought up the possibility that the CIA was involved with mind-control experimentation.

"Aha," he said, "so you're paranoid, huh?"

"Well, Tom, conspiracy and paranoia are not synonymous. Listen, I'll tell you about a real conspiracy theory."

"Okay," he said, "what?"

"Remember that horse, Ruffian, who broke her leg in a race, and then they shot her?"

"Yeah, what about it?"

"Well, you wanna know why they shot her?"

"Why?" he asked, furrowing his brow.

"Because she knew too much."

Snyder looked at his producer as if to say, "Who booked this flake?" Then he realized that I was putting him on, and he started laughing. To me, secretly peaking on mushrooms, it looked as though Tom Snyder was doing Dan Aykroyd doing Tom Snyder on *Saturday Night Live*, and his laughter sounded like a string of eerie musical notes.

At the time, Abbie Hoffman was on the lam, but this was November 30, and I had promised to wish him a happy birthday on the air, which I did.

"Where is he?" Snyder asked. "Maybe we can get him on the show."

"He's right there under your chair."

Back in my hotel room that night, still feeling very sensual from the mushrooms, I made love with a former girlfriend who was a masseuse, and later I asked her for a massage.

"Sure," she said, "but I'll have to charge you for that."

ALBERT ELLIS MEETS LENNY BRUCE

The recent death of groundbreaking psychologist Albert Ellis brought to mind his strong opposition to the censorship of pornography in general and of *Deep Throat* in particular.

"We all fantasize having an enjoyable meal at times," he said, "and that hardly interferes with our actual enjoyment of eating."

I first met Dr. Ellis in 1953, when I was managing editor of *The Independent*. One of my early tasks had been to write ads for the books we offered, including a couple by Ellis, *The Folklore of Sex* and *The American Sexual Tragedy*. His point of view was so against the grain of mainstream culture that I assumed he must have written articles that he couldn't get published. I contacted him, and he sent me seven such articles.

Ellis became a monthly columnist for *The Independent*. Editor Lyle Stuart had also become a book publisher, and he published a collection of columns by Ellis titled *Sex Without Guilt*. I wrote a parody called "Guilt Without Sex"—a sex manual for adolescents—for *Mad* magazine, but it was rejected because of its subject matter. I sold it to *Playboy* instead.

At the time *Mad* had already reached circulation of 1.25 million, mostly teens, and I said to publisher Bill Gaines, "I guess you don't want to change horses in midstream." He replied, "Not when the horse has a rocket up its ass." There was no satire magazine for adults in those days—this was in the late 1950s, before *National Lampoon* and *Spy*—so with the encouragement and mentoring of Stuart I launched my own publication, *The Realist*, and in 1959 Robert Anton Wilson and I interviewed Albert Ellis. At one point we got onto a tangent about the semantics of profanity.

"Take, for example," he said, "the campaign which I have been waging, with remarkable lack of success, for many years, in favor of the proper usage of the word *fuck*. My premise is that sexual intercourse, copulation, fucking or whatever you wish to call it, is normally, under almost all circumstances, a damned good thing. Therefore, we should rarely use it in a negative, condemnatory manner. Instead of denouncing someone by calling him "a fucking bastard," we should say, of course, that he is "an *un*fucking villain" (since *bastard*, too, is not necessarily a negative state and should not only be used pejoratively)."

"How about the famous Army saying, 'Fuck all of them but six and save them for the pallbearers.' There, *fuck* means *kill*."

"Yes, and it is wrongly used. It should be '*Un*fuck all of them but six.' Lots of times these words are used correctly, as when you say, 'I had a fucking good time.' That's quite accurate, since fucking, as I said before, is a good thing, and a good thing leads to a good time. But by the same token you should say, 'I had an *un*fucking *bad* time.'"

"I can see this scrawled on subway posters: *Unfuck You!*"

"Why not? It's fuckingly more logical that way, isn't it?"

Not that Ellis practiced what he preached. In keeping with his confrontational approach to patients, he asked one, "Do you know why your family is trying to control you? Because they're out of their fucking minds!"

Just when the issue of *The Realist* with the Ellis interview was published, Lenny Bruce—whom I had interviewed the previous month—came to New York for a midnight show at Town Hall. He called me that afternoon, and we met at the Hotel America in Times Square. At this point in Lenny's career, he was still using the euphemism *frig* on stage. Although the mass media were already translating his irreverence as that of a "sick comic," he had not yet been branded "filthy." I handed him the new issue of *The Realist* with the Albert Ellis interview. He was amazed that I could get away with publishing it.

"Are you telling me," he asked, "this is legal to sell on the newsstands?"

"Absolutely. The Supreme Court's definition of

obscenity is that it has to be material which appeals to your prurient interest."

Lenny magically produced an unabridged dictionary from the suitcase on his bed, and he looked up the word *prurient*.

"Itching," he mused. "What does that *mean*—that they can bust a novelty-store owner for selling itching powder along with the dribble glass and the whoopie cushion?"

"It's just their way of saying that something gets you horny."

Lenny closed the dictionary, clenching his jaw and nodding his head in affirmation of a new discovery. "So," he said, "it's against the law to get you horny." He asked me to give out copies of that issue of *The Realist* in front of Town Hall before his concert that night. Lenny brought a copy on stage and proceeded to talk about it. As a result, he was barred from performing there again. *Down Beat* magazine editorialized:

"What was Town Hall's objection to Bruce's recent midnight show there? Evidently it boiled down to embarrassment at the presence *outside the doors* of a group giving out free copies of a Greenwich Village magazine called *The Realist*. The magazine contained an interview with a psychologist on the semantics of a well-known four-letter word. Town Hall deemed the contents pornographic. Bruce is no longer welcome, though he had nothing to do with the magazine or the group giving it away."

"They'll book me again," Lenny said. "They made too much money on that concert. I'd have more respect for them if they *didn't* ever book me again. At least, it'd show they were keeping their word."

And he was right. They *did* book him again.

Ironically, the *New York Times* obituary of Albert Ellis stated that "he was called the Lenny Bruce of psychotherapy."

NORMAN MAILER'S FORESKIN

When Norman Mailer wrote his first novel, *The Naked and the Dead*, he used a euphemism—"fug"—for fuck, which of course is where The Fugs got their name. The first time I encountered Mailer, I asked if it was true that when he met actress Tallulah Bankhead, she said, "So you're the young man who doesn't know how to spell fuck." With a twinkle in his eye, he told me that he replied, "Yes, and you're the young woman who doesn't know how to."

I saw Mailer again at City Hall Park in New York at the height of the Cold War. We were both among a thousand citizens committing civil disobedience against the law that required us to seek shelter during an air raid drill. Umbrellas bearing the legend PORTABLE FALLOUT SHELTER were held up while the crowd sang "America the Beautiful."

As soon as the air raid siren sounded, the chief of police announced, "Officers, arrest those persons who do not seek shelter!" The cops seized those persons who were nearest to them, including Mailer. Then the all-clear siren sounded, and the rest of the protesters began to disperse.

When I originally launched *The Realist* in 1958, I requested an interview with Mailer. He declined, but in 1962, after I published an interview with Joseph Heller when *Catch 22* was published, Mailer called me. He was finally ready. We met at his home in Brooklyn Heights. Mailer sat in a chair, poised like a prizefighter. And I was his sparring partner.

In 1963, when I performed stand-up at Town Hall and introduced Heller in the audience, somebody else, a friend of his, stood up, but since the audience didn't know what Heller looked like, they applauded.

"That's not Joseph Heller," I said from the stage. "This is right out of *Catch 22*."

Then I introduced Mailer, and again somebody else stood up. This time it was a young woman

"I'm a friend of Norman's," she called out. "He couldn't come tonight."

"That's the story of his life," I responded. It was a cheap shot, but I couldn't resist. "He's writing another book about it," I added.

In my interview with Mailer, we had been talking about the mating process of two individuals. "It's mutually selective," he said. "You fall in together or go in together." Little did I dream that I would end up "falling in together" with that young woman in the audience, Jeanne Johnson. We got married at his home and had a daughter, Holly.

The last time I saw Mailer was in 2005 at Wordstock, the first annual Portland (Oregon) Book Festival, where I was invited to open for Mailer and then introduce him.

"The thing I most admire about Mailer," I said, "is a combination of his courage as a writer and how much he respects the craft. He writes in longhand with a number two pencil, he told me once, because it puts him in more direct contact with the paper that he's writing on, and I felt so guilty because I was still using a typewriter at the time. You remember typewriters. In fact, I have a niece who saw a manual typewriter, and she said, 'What's that for?' I explained, and she said, "Well, where do you plug it in?' 'You don't have to plug it in, you just push the keys.' And she said, 'That's awesome!'

"Anyway, one aspect of Norman Mailer's craft is that he chooses his words very carefully. Or, as he would say, 'One chooses one's words very carefully.' The thing that I recall, the words that he chose most carefully, of all the books he's written, was something that he said [43 years ago] when I asked him how he felt about circumcision. He thought for a moment, then he chose his words carefully and, with a twinkle in his eye—one of his main characteristics—he said, 'Well, I believe that if Jews didn't have circumcision, they would punch their babies in the nose and break them. . . .' "

When Mailer came on stage, walking with the aid of two canes because of a severe arthritic condition, he received a standing ovation. He eased himself onto a high chair behind the lectern.

"Gee, Paul, I didn't know how to start tonight," he said, "but maybe you got me going. Now, if I ever made that remark, that the reason Jews get circumcised is to keep them from breaking their babies' noses, all I can say is that I must have been down in the lower depths of a very bad marijuana trip. But I think, even at my worst, I couldn't really have said that. Paul is a master of hyperbole. He loves hyperbole, as for example when Lyndon Johnson 'attacked' the wound in JFK's head.

"At any rate, if I did say it, I would forgive myself now for having said it, because circumcision happens to be something that every Jewish male thinks about every day of his life. It makes us obsessive for a very simple reason. We don't know if it's an asset or a liability. And I'm not speaking of it lightly. I'm speaking of psychic castration that may make us smarter or it may not. We worry about things like that. So I will say categorically, that if I ever made that remark, I was out of my head, and to the best of my marijuana memory, I never made it. I want to thank you, Paul, for making that up and giving me a beginning tonight, and for warming up this audience. . . ."

One night a couple of years later, I had a dream that Mailer died. Now that Holly would be getting married, when I woke up I decided to send a note to tell him. But then I heard on NPR that he had died, and it was too late.

I also received this e-mail from an old friend, Sheila Campion:

"I just read that Norman Mailer died. I know you knew him. When my son was about 10 years old, I took him to see Mailer at Elliott Bay Bookstore in Seattle for a reading. We went after to have him sign his new book. He was very nice. He talked with us both and asked my son how things were, and asked if he could do anything for him. My son said, 'You could help me with my term paper.' Mailer laughed and said, 'Oh, no, my son already asked me, and I told *him* no too.' I will light a candle for him."

MOUNTAIN GIRL REMEMBERS ALBERT HOFMANN

On the day that the man who discovered LSD, Dr. Albert Hofmann, died at the age of 102, *The Onion* ostensibly asked people what they thought. "It's just like I tell my kids," replied one. "If you get involved with drugs, you're going to end up dead." The death of this renowned Swiss chemist also inspired David Letterman to share with his audience that same evening the fact that researchers have "combined LSD with birth control pills so you can take a trip without the kids." The *New York Times* obituary stated that in April 1943 Hofmann "accidentally ingested the substance that became known to the 1960s counterculture as acid." But the *Los Angeles Times* obituary stated that he had "accidentally gotten a trace amount of an experimental compound called lysergic acid diethylamide on his fingertips and taken the world's first acid trip."

And the accurate answer, in Hofmann's own words, from his book, *LSD: My Problem Child*: "How had I managed to absorb this material? Because of the known toxicity of ergot substances, I always maintained meticulously neat work habits. Possibly a bit of the LSD solution had contacted my fingertips during crystallization, and a trace of the substance was absorbed through the skin."

At first, he didn't know what caused his mysteriously scary and beautiful reactions. He tried breathing the solvents he had used, with no effect. But then, he said in an interview on his hundredth birthday, "LSD spoke to me. He came to me and said, 'You must find me.' He told me, 'Don't give me to the pharmacologist, he won't find anything.'"

Four weeks before his death, Carolyn Garcia had given a speech at the World Psychedelic Forum in Basel, where Hofmann lived, and she was invited to meet him.

"He was so sweet to me," she recalls. "Chatted and joked about musicians and black market LSD, chocolate and cherry trees, instructed me very seriously about the importance of hanging upside down every day, to improve the blood flow to the brain." He discussed with an old friend, Juri Styk, "whether Sandoz Laboratories would approach other chemical companies to make some LSD for the new studies being conducted in Europe. Important studies, on LSD and dying, cancer relief and spiritual psychological benefits of its use for rebalancing people in crisis. 'Long overdue,' they said."

Carolyn asked Hofmann if the purification of LSD was a long process. He denied it and said, "LSD is very easy to make, you just do the recipe, and if it crystallizes, that is it, it's done and very pure. No need to do anything else." She told him a little about the Grateful Dead, "and he lit up and said he had 'always been hearing about them, they played existential music, yes? And from small beginnings, it got large?'

"With the help of LSD, the energy and telepathic melted together as they played. He understood that. He asked about Jerry. And Juri reminded him about the Acid Tests, and he lit up again and said, 'Oh, yes, the Acid Tests, and the Grateful Dead played there long also? And you were there?' And I smiled, yes, and pulled out the Acid Test diploma I had made for him. I presented it in the usual fashion, saying that he had proven beyond doubt that he had fulfilled all the requirements and had certainly passed the Acid Test, and had earned this Acid Test diploma."

When she left, Hofmann "smiled and asked me to come back, and bring the sun, please. The wind was whipping the snow out of the trees as silent puffs of feathers. The walkway to the car was thick with ice. A few cat tracks showed the way. I didn't get to meet the cat, who sleeps on the doctor's bed since his wife passed away. Now where's the cat sleeping tonight?"

The United States government banned LSD in October 1966, and other countries followed. Hofmann insisted that this was not fair. He argued that the drug wasn't addictive and campaigned for the ban to be lifted so that LSD could be used in medical research. In December 2007, Swiss authorities decided to allow the drug to be used in a psychotherapy research project.

"For me," Hofmann told Swiss TV, "this is a very big wish come true. I always wanted to see LSD get its proper place in medicine."

On the day of his death, the Albert Hofmann Foundation declared that "Dr. Hofmann's discoveries have touched countless people and brought tremendous change to the world in more ways than can be counted. We are very glad that Dr. Hofmann could still witness the early stages of new studies with LSD that will start in Switzerland in the near future."

MICHAEL ROSSMAN: A TOUCH OF SATIVA

You may never have heard of Michael Rossman, though he became a countercultural inspiration to young people during the 1960s when he was an organizer of the Free Speech Movement, which began at the Berkeley campus of the University of California—fighting a ban on political activism—and rapidly spread to colleges around the country. He served as a social and political activist for decades, but didn't take himself as seriously as the causes he fought for.

He spent nine weeks behind bars, where he was assigned to garbage detail. However, such punishment didn't bother him the way his jailers had intended, since he happened not to have a sense of smell, a fact he disclosed in his first book, *The Wedding Within the War*. His other books include *On Learning and Social Change* and *New Age Blues:*

On the Politics of Consciousness. He was conceived during the Spanish Civil War and translated some of the greatest poetry from that era.

On May 3, 2008, nine days before his death from leukemia at the age of 68, Rossman showed up at the Bolshevik Cafe in Berkeley's Red Finn Hall, wearing a robber's-type mask. He had worked with Arnie Passman on the Golden Jubilee of the Peace Symbol celebration in February, and now asked him if he could read a poem he had written as a way of saying good-bye to family and friends. It was the two-hundredth anniversary of the event in Madrid during Napoleon's Peninsular War that had inspired Goya to paint his classic *The Shootings of May Third*, perhaps Spain's most famous painting, and the 1958 inspiration for the peace symbol. Michael took the stage, accompanied by his oxygen tank, and he proceeded to read his poem "Dear Body, Dear Body Mine":

> Thank you for bearing me
> through the world so sensitively
> so vibrantly so long
>
> Thank you thighs for carrying me
> to the top of Shasta to see Heather
> doff her thermals and stand gloriously
> one-breasted in the snow
> as butterflies streamed above
>
> Thank you intricate apparatus
> of my inner ears for allowing me
> to hear Sibelius, to tell oak
> from bay in the night wind's rustle

and the slither of skink from alligator
lizard in the day

Thank you larynx for not cracking
too much when I finally learned
to sing among the chidren, for letting
me roar and whisper in play personae

Thank you stomach for taking apart
everything I fed you, the maggots
and stuffed jalapeños as well
as the strawberries and leeks
and never complaining

Thank you teeth for cracking
so many nuts before cracking,
for not shifting when some
fell away, for your lucid chatter
when ice wind whipped off the lake

Thank you lips for shaping
the pure sounds in my flute's throat
anyway even if I never
taught you right

Thank you eyes for echoing
my grandfather, for changing
like deep waters, for reading
the condensed *OED* [*Oxford English Dictionary*]
    unaided
past fifty, for seeing so much
so clearly after objective

refractive tests said that
was impossible, for showing me
fifty thousand hues inside "green"
and my granddaughter's visage
ecstatic and the untold fleeting
faces of my lovers and the print
in pulp magazines under the bedcovers
in the flashlit transgressions
that left my parents smiling

Thank you hair for keeping me
warm, for letting me play with
appearance, for comforting
my touch no matter how ratty
your length looked for so long,
for coming back in downy second
life after the chemo

Thank you lungs for providing
such rich oxygenation all along
beyond the norm, for allowing
the touch of sativa to lift my
spirit in play, for forgiving
so many insults, for letting me
lug down malachite breccias
from high on Mt. Majuba
before I went in hospital

Thank you clever fingers
for unknotting the backlash
on so many reels, for guiding
my cramped and lucid pen,

dancing on strings and tone-
holes, digging grubs within
punky wood, for tracing the knots
of energy under my dear friends'
shoulderblades, unknitting them,
standing by to let my energy
fingers go deeper yet in release

Thank you tongue for remembering
my mother's nipples so well,
for savoring the flavors
of a hundred lands, for surprising
me with the profundity
of still-touching with Anne's

Thank you skin for so loving
the sun's benediction, Karen's gentle
and shivery touch, the aftermath
of stinging-nettle that tingles
in you since yesterday's
creek-walk with Sage, the lash
of brambles across my unguarded
ankles, the cut of milkteeth that left
such permanent lacy palimpsests
across my forearms from sparring
full-out with Bull and Flux, each sliver,
each incautious slash, each rasp
of my knee on the wrestling mat
that left you joyous as a Border Collie
herding lost sheep to do
what you best could, my healing
integument

Thank you my soles
who carried me unguarded to
the top of Whitney with my son,
who gave me gave me such pleasure
naked on the pavement the sandy
beach the sharps of crumbled shale
feeling so directly the contours
of my world, endorphins zinging
my spirits in music from your random
pianos of pressed points

Thank you o my testicles
for swelling so painfully
in youthful tease and denial,
for squirming and lifting and
lowering your precious cargo,
for your mechanisms of random
recombination yielding the gametes
joining with Karen's to produce
such remarkable beings as our sons

Thank you my penis
my pretty dependable fool
for giving me such pleasures
and release without complications
by myself for so long, for inviting
her admiration and fondling and squirming pleasure,
the deep bonding persistent
whatever your mood

And thank you my brain, you elegant
transducer of my nimble mind,

glorious, retentive, fast-calculating,
ineffable-glimpsing, sharp-focusing,
field-grasping, proliferative
of metaphor and shades of feeling,
luxuriously playful, shaded
by awe, responding to almost
everything I asked and more
than I knew to want or
recognize, oh how you will
be missed and honored in wonder
by whatever of me may persist

Thank you all, thank you only
as one for my integral being in this life.

In 2007, celebrating the fortieth anniversary of the Summer of Love, Michael reminisced about the counterculture and pot smoking:

"The thing about weed and political action, in that era, when you sucked on a joint, you inhaled not simply some smoke, but you inhaled this whole complex of cultural attitudes, not only opposition to the Vietnam War, but a liking for Madras bedspreads, an inclination to taste new and interesting foods, to feel less guilty about cutting class, to disrespect authority more because they were trying to make you a criminal for having these experiences and changes of perspective. When you made millions of young people criminals this way, on the narrow issue of whether they could put this plant's smoke or that plant's smoke in their bodies, you corrupted their attitudes about a whole lot in the culture.

"This was a time when still in order to smoke the

marijuana we locked the front door, we turned out all the lights, crowded in the bathroom and stood around the toilet ready to flush if the cops were going to knock on the door. We got high, went out and looked at M.C. Escher and listened to Bach with a new ear. So when the Haight emerged as a place where people smoked marijuana openly, it was a deeper kind of transgression and statement of liberation than can be understood in this day or by people who didn't live through that time. God knows it drove the authorities nuts."

I once quoted Timothy Leary's premise that demonstrations against the Vietnam War "played right onto the game-boards of the administration and the police alike, and that students could shake up the establishment much more if they would just stay in their rooms and change their nervous systems." But, I wrote, "It wasn't really a case of either-or. You could protest *and* explore your 13-billion-celled mind simultaneously. During the mass imprisonment of Free Speech Movement demonstrators, a Bible that had been soaked in acid solution easily made its way into the jail cells, with students just eating those pages up, getting high on Deuteronomy, tripping out on Exodus."

The last time I saw Michael Rossman was in 2004 at the fortieth anniversary of the Free Speech Movement. He had asked several participants whether that was a true story about an LSD-soaked Bible being smuggled into jail, verifying that it was only a false rumor. I promised him that I would find a way to retract it. And now I've kept that promise.

GEORGE CARLIN HAS LEFT THE GREEN ROOM

In December 1962, when Lenny Bruce was arrested for obscenity at the Gate of Horn in Chicago, the police broke open his candy bars, looking for dope. They checked the IDs of audience members, including George Carlin, who told the cops, "I don't believe in IDs." Then they arrested *him* for disorderly conduct, dragged him along by the seat of his pants and hoisted him into the police wagon.

"What are *you* doing here?" Lenny asked.

"I didn't want to show them my ID."

"You *schmuck*," said Lenny.

Lenny and Carlin had similar points of view—for example, they were both outspoken about the decriminalization of drugs—and they were both self-educated, but their working styles were different. Lenny didn't write his material, it evolved on stage, whereas Carlin *did* write all his routines and then memorized 'em. Although both were unbelievers as far as religion was concerned, Lenny came from a Jewish background, and Carlin came from an Irish Catholic background.

Susie Bright, who first heard Carlin when she was in seventh grade, recalls playing his *Class Clown* album for her mother, "a woman whose first twenty years were entirely dominated by the Irish Catholic Church—and it was a comic exorcism for her. She peed in her pants! She was cured in one LP [long-playing vinyl record]!"

Socrates said, "Know thyself"; Norman Mailer said, "Be thyself"; and the 1960s counterculture said, "Change thyself." Carlin—who had entered show business in the late 1950s, wearing a suit and tie, performing traditional stand-up schtick—started surfing on that wave. He reinvented himself visually—jeans, T-shirt, beard, ponytail—and later acknowledged that smoking pot had really helped him to fine-tune his material.

"My comedy changed because my life changed," he said. "The act followed what was going on in me. Humor is very subjective, and what I was doing on stage didn't match up with what was going on in my life or the country—1967 was the Summer of Love, it was the height of the cultural revolution—love, peace, free sex, all crested that summer. Everything was changing. I was playing big shows like Jack Paar and Ed Sullivan, but inside I was anti-authority and I hated that shit. Parents might not have been able to relate, so I went to the kids. I was using my act to further my ideas about the times."

Carlin was a generous friend, and such a sweet man. When I performed in Los Angeles, he sent a limousine to pick me up at the airport, and I stayed at his home. Several years later, I opened for him at the Warner-Grand Theater in San Pedro, California. We were hanging around in his dressing room, where he was nibbling from a vegetable plate. I watched as he continued to be genuinely gracious with every fan who stopped by. If they wanted his autograph, he would gladly sign his name. If they wanted to be photographed with him, he would assume the pose. If they wanted to have a little chat, he indulged them with congeniality.

"You really show respect for everybody," I observed.

"Well," he responded, "that's just the way *I* would want to be treated."

As a performer, Carlin was uncompromising, knowing that his audience trusted him not to be afraid of offending them. In fact, he was excited by that possibility. The day before one of his live HBO specials, he called and told me to be sure and watch, because he would devote the first ten minutes of his performance to the subject of abortion.

Carlin had long been vocal in support of the right to smoke and ingest various drugs, and posed this rhetorical question: "Why are there no recreational drugs in suppository form?" I was pleased to inform him that teenage girls have been experimenting with tampons soaked in vodka, inserting them vaginally or rectally as a way of getting intoxicated without their parents detecting booze on their breath.

No matter what else Richard Nixon accomplished in his lifetime, his obituaries always mentioned him as the first American president to resign, and no matter what else George Carlin accomplished in *his* lifetime, his obits will always connect him with the Supreme Court ruling on "The Seven Words You Can't Say on Television."

When asked in the Green Room at the Warner Grand Theater by producer Dan Pasley why he didn't include the word "nigger" in that list, Carlin replied, "There's nothing funny about it—that really *is* a dirty word—but repressed words about sexual functions and bodily parts were truly funny. I had only been thinking about the 'dirty' words in terms of sex and bodily functions, and how uptight these religious freaks have made us. That's fun, that's some funny shit."

Carlin provided an introduction to one of my books, *Murder at the Conspiracy Convention*. Referring to the 1960s, he wrote: "As America entered the Magic Decade, I was leading a double life. I had been a rule-bender and law-breaker since first grade. A highly developed disregard for authority got me kicked out of three schools, the altar boys, the choir, summer camp, the Boy Scouts and the Air Force.

I didn't trust the police or the government, and I didn't like bosses of any kind. I had become a pot smoker at 13 (1950), an unheard-of act in an old-fashioned Irish neighborhood. It managed to get me through my teens. . . .

"My affection for pot continued and my disregard for standard values increased, but they lagged behind my need to succeed. The Playboy Club, Merv Griffin, Ed Sullivan and the Copacabana were all part of a path I found uncomfortable but necessary during the early 1960s. But as the decade churned along and the country changed, I did too. Despite working in 'establishment' settings, as a veteran malcontent I found myself hanging out in coffee houses and folk clubs with others who were out-of-step people who fell somewhere between beatnik and hippie. Hair got longer, clothes got stranger, music got better. It became more of a strain for me to work for straight audiences. I took acid and mescaline. My sense of being on the outside intensified. I changed.

"All through this period I was sustained and motivated by *The Realist*, Paul Krassner's incredible magazine of satire, revolution and just plain disrespect. It arrived every month, and with it, a fresh supply of inspiration. I can't overstate how important it was to me at the time. It allowed me to see that others who disagreed with the American consensus were busy expressing those feelings and using risky humor to do so. Paul's own writing, in particular, seemed daring and adventurous to me; it took big chances and made important arguments in relentlessly funny ways. I felt, down deep, that maybe I had some of that in me, too; that maybe I could be using my skills to better express my beliefs. *The Realist* was the inspiration that kept pushing me to the next level; there was no way I could continue reading it and remain the same."

You can imagine how incredibly honored I felt.

At a private memorial for family and friends, Carlin's daughter Kelly read from his burial instructions, written on May 1, 1990:

"Upon my death, I wish to be cremated. The disposition of my ashes (dispersal at sea, on land or in the air) shall be determined by my surviving family (wife and daughter) in accordance with their knowledge of my prejudices and philosophies regarding geography and spirituality. Under no circumstances are my ashes to be retained by anyone or buried in a particular location. The eventual dispersal can be delayed for any reasonable length of time required to reach a decision, but not to exceed one month following my death.

"I wish no public service of any kind. I wish no religious service of any kind. I prefer a private gathering at my home, attended by friends and family members who shall be determined by my surviving family (wife and daughter). It should be extremely informal, they should play rhythm and blues music, and they should laugh a lot. Vague references to spirituality (secular) will be permitted."

Kelly added, "There will be no mention of God allowed" and "No one will be allowed to say that 'George is now smiling down at us from Heaven above.'"

Carlin once told an audience of children how to be a class clown as a way of attracting attention. "I didn't start out with fake heart attacks in the aisle," he explained. Ah, if only that's what he was doing *this* time.

But a reporter did once ask him how he wanted to die.

"I'd like to explode spontaneously in someone's living room," he replied. "That, to me, is the way to go out."

And, through his CDs, DVDs and books, George Carlin does indeed continue to explode spontaneously in living rooms across the country.

5.

FREEDOM'S JUST ANOTHER WORD

EXCLUSIVE INTERVIEW WITH MICHAEL PHELPS

Q: What've you learned from this whole nuclear *bong* explosion?

A: I learned how fast you can go from being an international hero to being a reference in a joke on a late-night talk show. I heard Jay Leno say, "You know what really did Tom Daschle in? It turns out there are now pictures of him partying with Michael Phelps." And David Letterman: "I don't want to just ruin everybody's day, but there is discouraging news everywhere. Unemployment is high. Foreclosure rate is high. Michael Phelps is high."

Q: Well, that's what happens when your *profile* is so high. But your coach said that you would learn from the experience.

A: I learned that it was my own fault. I was so busy getting treated like a horny Jesus that I forgot that there could possibly be a Judas in the room. A greedy Judas with a cell phone camera. *That* was my mistake. *That's* what I regret. *That's* what will never happen again. I mean what happens in South Carolina *doesn't* stay in South Carolina. It ends up in Tabloid Hell And Judas got a friggin' hundred thousand dollars to play with.

Q: In England, yet. And then it comes back here to the States and drops in the lap of the Kellogg Empire. I called their headquarters, and there was an automatic message: "Press one to leave a comment about Michael Phelps—"
A: They were afraid that my image would pollute *their* image. That my brand would damage *their* brand. But the truth is, I actually felt relieved. I had been like a whore. Selling my soul instead of renting my body. And Tony the Tiger was my pimp. A nutritionist told me that the absolutely worst thing to have in your diet is sugar-coated cereal. And there I was, pushing Frosted Flakes—and it's friggin' *addictive*, man—I was peddling a dangerous breakfast cereal to innocent little kids. And those Kellogg PR people were worried about what message was *my* behavior sending? What message does dealing *junk food* send?

Q: But this whole thing also served to open up dialogue. I saw Whoopi Goldberg on *The View*—she said, "I smoked weed," and most of the audience applauded. And don't forget, that's Middle America.
A: Y'know what I'd *really* like to do? When I was like 12 years old, there was this issue of *Time* magazine with Ellen DeGeneres on the cover, and she's saying, "Yep, I'm Gay." So now *I* wanna be on the cover of *Newsweek*, smoking a joint and saying, "Yep, I'm Stoned." I wanna be the poster boy for the decriminalization of marijuana. If I'm supposed to be a role model, it would be great to inspire tokers to come out of *their* closets. Listen, did you know that almost

one out of every three Americans have smoked marijuana? There's strength in numbers, although everybody's afraid of losing their jobs, but *they* know that the real harm comes from the ridiculous, insane laws, not from the weed.

Q: And don't forget the vicious propaganda. Did you happen to see a commercial by the Office of National Drug Control Policy? It features a woman saying, "Hey, not trying to be your mom, but there aren't many jobs out there for pot-heads." Your mother is the principal of a middle school, right? What do you think *her* reaction would be to your pro-pot crusade?

A: Oh, I'm sure she wouldn't be very supportive. In fact, she'd be very upset. She would grit her teeth and she'd say, "Michael, you are *grounded* for three weeks!"

THERE ARE NO ATHEISTS IN THE WHITE HOUSE

Whenever anybody claims that God talks directly to them, I think they're totally delusional. George Bush is no exception. Not only was he told by his senior adviser, Karen Hughes, not to refer to terrorists as "folks," but Bush was also being prompted by God Him-Her-or-Itself: "God would tell me, 'George, go and end the tyranny in Iraq.' And I did." As if he was only following divine orders.

In *The Fall of the House of Bush: The Untold Story of How a Band of True Believers Seized the Executive Branch, Started the Iraq War, and Still Imperils America's Future*, Craig Unger writes: "Conventional wisdom has it that George W. Bush became a 'born-again' Christian in the summer of 1985, after extended private talks with Reverend Billy Graham. As recounted by Bush himself in *A Charge to Keep: My Journey to the White House*, a ghostwritten autobiography prepared for the 2000 presidential campaign, Bush and Graham went for a walk along the rugged Maine shore, past the Boony Wild Pool where Bush had skinny-dipped as a child. 'I knew I was in the presence of a great man,' Bush wrote. 'He was like a magnet; I felt drawn to seek something different. He didn't lecture or admonish; he shared warmth and concern. Billy Graham didn't make you feel guilty; he made you feel loved. Over the course of that weekend, Rev. Graham planted a mustard seed in my soul, a seed that grew over the next year. He led me to the path, and I began walking.'

"There's just one problem with Bush's account of his conversion experience: It's not true. For one thing, when Billy Graham was asked abut the episode by NBC's Brian Williams, he declined to corroborate Bush's account. 'I've heard others say that [I converted Bush], and people have written it, but I cannot say that,' Graham said. 'I was with him and I used to teach the Bible at Kennebunkport to the Bush family when he was a younger man, but I never feel that I in any way turned his life around.'

"Even if one doesn't accept Graham's candid response, there's another good reason to believe that the account in Bush's book is fiction. Mickey Herskowitz, a sportswriter for the *Houston Chronicle* who became close friends with the Bush family and was originally contracted to ghost-write *A Charge to Keep*, recalled interviewing Bush about it when he was doing research for the book. 'I remember asking him about the famous meeting at Kennebunkport with the Reverend Billy Graham,' Herskowitz said. 'And you know what? He couldn't remember a single word that passed between them.' Herskowitz was so stunned by

Bush's memory lapse that he began prompting him. 'It was so unlikely he wouldn't remember anything Billy Graham said, especially because that was a defining moment in his life. So I asked, 'Well, Governor, would he have said something like, "Have you gotten right with God?"' According to Herskowitz, Bush was visibly taken aback and bristled at the suggestion. 'No,' Bush replied. 'Billy Graham isn't going to ask you a question like that.'

"Herskowitz met with Bush about twenty times for the project and submitted about ten chapters before Bush's staff, working under director of communications Karen Hughes, who took control of it. But when Herskowitz finally read *A Charge to Keep*, he was stunned by its contents. 'Anyone who is writing a memoir of George Bush for campaign purposes knew you had to have some glimpse of what passed between Bush and Billy Graham,' he said. But Hughes and her team had changed a key part. 'It had Graham asking Bush, 'George, are right with God?' In other words, Herskowitz's question to Bush was now coming out of Billy Graham's mouth. 'Karen Hughes picked it off the tape,' said Herskowitz."

◆ ◆ ◆

In July 2003, during a meeting with Palestinian Prime Minister Mahmoud Abbas, Bush told the newly elected leader, "God told me to strike at Al-Qaeda and I struck them, and then He instructed me to strike at Saddam, which I did. And now I am determined to solve the problem in the Middle East. If you help me, I will act, and if not, the elections will come and I will have to focus on them."

Abu Bakar Bashir, an Islamic cleric and accused terrorist

leader, has said that "America's aim in attacking Iraq is to attack Islam, so it is justified for Muslims to target America to defend themselves." That's exactly interchangeable with this description of Bush by an unidentified family member, quoted in the *Los Angeles Times*: "George sees [the war on terror] as a religious war. His view is that they are trying to kill the Christians. And the Christians will strike back with more force and more ferocity than they will ever know."

Apparently, religious bigotry runs in the family. Bush's father, the former president: "I don't know that atheists should be considered citizens, nor should they be considered patriots. This is one nation under God." And before him, there was Ronald Reagan: "For the first time ever, everything is in place for the Battle of Armageddon and the Second Coming of Christ." Not to mention Reagan's Secretary of the Interior, James Watt, responsible for national policy on the environment: "We don't have to protect the environment—the Second Coming is at hand."

In 1966, Lyndon Johnson told the Austrian ambassador that the deity "comes and speaks to me about two o'clock in the morning when I have to give the word to the boys, and I get the word from God whether to bomb or not." So maybe there's some kind of theological tradition going on in the White House.

But if these leaders are *not* delusional, then they're deceptive. And in order to deceive others, one must first deceive oneself until self-deception morphs into virtual reality. In any case, we have our religious fanatics, and they have theirs. In September 2007, on the eve of the sixth anniversary of 9/11, Osama bin Laden warned the American people that they should reject their capitalist way of life and embrace Islam to end the Iraq war, or else his followers would "escalate the killing and fighting against you."

When Ann Coulter—former Justice Department attorney and Senate aide, now a professional reactionary and Stepford pundit—was a guest on CNBC's *The Big Idea*, host Donny Deutsch asked her what an ideal country would be like, and she replied that it would be one in which everybody was a Christian. "We just want Jews to be perfected," she explained. As for Muslims, two days after the terrorist attacks on 9/11, she wrote in *National Review Online*, "We should invade their countries, kill their leaders and convert them to Christianity."

And so it came to pass that, after four American mercenaries—oops, I mean contractors—were slaughtered in Fallujah, and consequently U.S. Marines bombed mosques where weapons of individual destruction had been stored, they also shot bullets into copies of the Koran. Which only increased the perception of a religious war that Muslims must avenge.

Indeed, General William Boykin, Deputy Undersecretary of Defense for Intelligence, said that "George Bush was not elected by a majority of the voters in the United States, he was appointed by God." Discussing the battle against a Muslim warlord in Somalia, Boykin explained, "I knew my God was bigger than his. I knew that my God was a real God and his was an idol." He also said, "Our spiritual enemy will only be defeated if we come against them in the name of Jesus." And, "Satan wants to destroy this nation, he wants to destroy us as a nation, and he wants to destroy us as a Christian army."

In May 2009, Jeremy Scahill blogged: "In a video

obtained by Al Jazeera, Lt.-Col. Gary Hensley, chief of the U.S. military chaplains in Afghanistan, is seen telling soldiers that as followers of Jesus Christ, they all have a responsibility 'to be witnesses for him. The special forces guys—they hunt men basically. We do the same thing as Christians, we hunt people for Jesus. We do, we hunt them down.' U.S. soldiers 'had [bibles translated into the two dominant languages of the overwhelmingly Muslim population] specially printed and shipped to Afghanistan... What these soldiers have been doing may well be in direct violation of the U.S. Constitution, their professional codes and the regulations in place for all forces in Afghanistan.' The U.S. military officially forbids 'proselytising of any religion, faith or practice.' But, as Al Jajeera reports, 'The chaplains appear to have found a way around the regulation known as General Order Number One. Capt. Emmit Furner, a military chaplain, says to the gathering, *Do we know what it means to proselytize?* An unidentified soldier replies, *It is General Order Number One. But . . . you can't proselytize but you can give gifts.*' Trying to convert Muslims to any other faith is a crime in Afghanistan."

With provocation like that, who needs friendly fire?

◆ ◆ ◆

George Bush once proclaimed, "God is not neutral," which is the antithesis of my own spiritual path, my own peculiar relationship with the universe—based on the notion that God is *totally* neutral—though I've learned that whatever people believe in, works for them.

My own belief in a deity disappeared when I was 13. I was working early mornings in a candy store in our apartment building. My job was to insert different sections of the newspaper into the main section. On the day after the United States dropped the first atomic bomb on Hiroshima, I would read that headline over and over and over again while I was working. That afternoon, I told God I couldn't believe in him anymore, because—even though he was supposed to be a loving and all-powerful being—he had allowed such devastation to happen. And then I heard the voice of God:

"*ALLOWED? WHY DO YOU THINK I GAVE HUMANS FREE WILL?*"

"Okay, well, I'm exercising my free will to believe that you don't exist."

"*ALL RIGHT, PAL, IT'S YOUR LOSS!*"

At least we would remain on speaking terms. But I knew it was a game. I enjoyed the paradox of developing a dialogue with a being whose reality now ranked with that of Santa Claus. Our previous relationship had instilled in me a touchstone of objectivity that could still serve to help keep me honest. I realized, though, that whenever I prayed, I was only talking to myself.

The only thing I can remember from my entire college education is a definition of philosophy as "the rationalization of life." For my term paper, I decided to write a dialogue between Plato and an atheist. On a whim, I looked up Atheism in the Manhattan phone book, and there it was: "Atheism, American Association for the Advancement of." I went to their office for background material.

The AAAA sponsored the Ism Forum, where anybody could speak about any "ism" of their choice. I invited a few acquaintances to meet me there. The event was held in a dingy hotel ballroom. There was a small platform with a podium at one end of the room and heavy wooden folding chairs lined around the perimeter. My favorite speaker declared the Eleventh Commandment: "Thou shalt not take thyself too goddamned seriously." Taking that as my unspoken theme, I got up and parodied the previous speakers. The folks there were mostly middle-aged and elderly. They seemed to relish the notion of fresh young blood in their movement.

However, my companions weren't interested in staying. If I had left with them that evening in 1953, the rest of my life could have taken a totally different path. Instead, I went along with a group to a nearby cafeteria, where I learned about the New York Rationalist Society. A whole new world of disbelief was opening up to me. That Saturday night I went to their meeting. The emcee was a former circus performer who entertained his fellow rationalists by putting four golf balls into his mouth. He also recommended an anti-censorship paper, *The Independent*.

The next week, I went to their office to subscribe and get back issues. I ended up with a part-time job, stuffing envelopes for a dollar an hour. My apprenticeship had begun. The editor, Lyle Stuart, was the most dynamic individual I'd ever met. His integrity was such that if he possessed information that he had a vested interest in keeping quiet—say, corruption involving a corporation in which he owned stock—it would become top priority for him to publish. Lyle became my media mentor, my unrelenting guru and my closest friend. He was responsible for the launch of *The Realist*. The masthead announced, "Freethought Criticism and Satire."

In 1962, when abortion was still illegal, I published an anonymous interview with the late Dr. Robert Spencer, a humane abortionist who was known as "The Saint." Patients came to his office in Ashland, Pennsylvania, from around the country. He had been performing abortions for forty years, started out charging $5, and never charged more than $100. Ashland was a small town, and Dr. Spencer's work was not merely tolerated, the community *depended* on it. The hotel, the restaurant, the dress shop—all thrived on the extra business that came from his out-of-town patients. He built facilities at his clinic for patients of color who weren't allowed to obtain overnight lodgings elsewhere in Ashland.

After the interview was published, I began to get phone calls from scared female voices. They were all in desperate search of a safe abortionist. Even a nurse couldn't find one. It was preposterous that they should have to seek out the editor of a satirical magazine, but their quest so far had been futile, and they simply didn't know where to turn. With Dr. Spencer's permission, I referred them to him. I had never intended to become an underground abortion referral service, but it wasn't going to stop just because in the next issue of *The Realist* there would be an interview with someone else.

A few years later, state police raided Dr. Spencer's clinic and arrested him. He remained out of jail only by the grace of political pressure from those he'd helped. He was finally forced to retire from his practice, but I continued mine, referring callers to other physicians he had recommended. Eventually, I was subpoenaed by district attorneys in two cities to appear before grand juries investigating criminal charges against abortionists. On both occasions, I refused to testify, and each time the D.A. tried to frighten me into cooperating with the threat of arrest.

Bronx D.A. (now Judge) Burton Roberts told me that his staff had found an abortionist's financial records, which showed all the money that I had received, but he would grant me immunity from prosecution if I cooperated with the grand jury. He extended his hand as a gesture of trust. "That's not true," I said, refusing to shake hands. If I *had* ever accepted any money, I'd have no way of knowing that he was bluffing.

At this point, attorney Gerald Lefcourt filed a suit on my behalf, challenging the constitutionality of the abortion law. He pointed out that the D.A. had no power to investigate the violation of an unconstitutional law, and therefore he could not force me to testify. In 1970, I became the only plaintiff in the first lawsuit to declare the abortion laws unconstitutional in New York State. Later, various women's groups joined the suit, and ultimately the New York legislature repealed the criminal sanctions against abortion, prior to the Supreme Court decision in *Roe v. Wade*.

Now we had a Republican candidate for president, Mitt Romney, who wanted to overturn *Roe v. Wade*. Yet, in 1994, when he was running for the Senate, he came out in favor of choice for women. Freelance journalist Suzan Mazur reveals that he admitted to Mormon feminist Judith Dushku that "the Brethren" in Salt Lake City *told* him he could take a pro-choice position, and that in fact he probably *had* to in order to win in a liberal state like Massachusetts. Pandering trumps religious belief.

Three presidential wannabes raised their hands during a Republican "debate" to signify that they didn't believe in evolution, although one of them, Mike Huckabee, admitted, "I don't know if the world was created in six days, I wasn't there." He has also said that, "If there was ever an occasion for someone to have argued against the death penalty, I think Jesus could have done so on the cross and said, 'This is an unjust punishment and I deserve clemency.'"

Huckabee's fellow creationist candidate, Tom Tancredo, asserted that bombing holy Muslim sites would serve as a good "deterrent" to prevent Islamic fundamentalists from attacking the United States. This notion of a pre-emptive assault made it into a Latino-oriented comic strip, *La Cucaracha* by Lalo Alcaraz: On TV, a narrator was saying, "You're watching *The U.S.'s Greatest Surprise Attacks* on the Distorted History Channel. Colorado Congressman Tom Tancredo issued a top-secret warning: 'The U.S. should nuke Islam's holy places!'" The TV viewer responds, "It is wrong to threaten nations with terror—unless Tom Tancredo does it." In a previous strip, from a car radio: "President Bush has taken to calling himself the inelegant 'Commander Guy.' May we suggest the more graceful 'Dictator Dude?'"

◆ ◆ ◆

Here are some quotes from various state constitutions. *Arkansas*: "No person who denies the being of a God shall hold any office." *Mississippi*: "No person who denies the existence of a Supreme Being shall hold any office in this state." *North Carolina*: "The following persons shall be disqualified for office: First, any person who shall deny the being of Almighty God." *South Carolina*: "No person shall be eligible to the office of Governor who denies the existence of the Supreme Being." *Tennessee*: "No person who denies the being of God, or a future state of rewards and punishments, shall hold any office in the civil department of this state." *Texas*: "Nor shall any one be excluded from holding office on account of his religious sentiments, provided he acknowledge the existence of a Supreme Being."

Rick Warren, pastor of America's fourth-largest church, told his congregation, "I could not vote for an atheist, because an atheist says, 'I don't need God.'"

In 2006, the Secular Coalition of America offered a $1,000 prize to anyone who identified the highest-ranking nontheist public official in the country. Almost sixty members of Congress were nominated, out of which twenty-two confided that didn't believe in a Supreme Being, but they wanted their disbelief kept secret. Only Pete Stark admitted that he was a nonbeliever, and in 2007, he became the first member of Congress ever to identify himself publicly as a nonbeliever.

In the week following that announcement, he received more than 5,000 e-mails from around the globe, almost all congratulating him for his courage. "Like our nation's founders," he stated, "I strongly support the separation of church and state. I look forward to working with the Secular Coalition to stop the promotion of narrow religious beliefs in science, marriage contracts, the military and the provision of social services." In 2008, he was elected to his nineteenth term with 76.5 percent of the votes.

In the race that year for the Senate in North Carolina, Elizabeth Dole approved a TV commercial criticizing her rival, former Sunday School teacher Kay Hagan, for ostensibly saying "There is no God," when it was really someone else's voice. Fortunately, Dole was defeated—most likely as a reaction to her bearing such false witness—but the implication was that Hagan (who sued for defamation) would have lost if she actually *had* been an atheist.

Barry Lynn, director of Americans United for the Separation of Church and State, believes that the "God supports Bush" theme held great currency among Bush's base because Bush wanted it to. "It is a belief the president encouraged, and that Karl Rove has encouraged," says Lynn. "It is, I think, extremely dangerous for people to believe that God is a Republican or a Democrat or a Naderite or even a Libertarian."

And Sam Harris, the author of *The End of Faith*, states that, "At a time when Muslim doctors and engineers stand accused of attempting atrocities in the expectation of supernatural reward, when the Catholic Church still preaches the sinfulness of condom use in villages devastated by AIDS, when the president of the United States repeatedly vetoes the most promising medical research for religious reasons, much depends on the scientific community presenting a united front against the forces of unreason."

A recent survey concluded that 59 percent of Americans think that any president of the United States should be "deeply religious." A Gallup poll indicated that 53 percent of respondents said they wouldn't vote for an otherwise well-qualified atheist. Another survey found that 61 percent would be less likely to support a presidential candidate who did not believe in God, and 45 percent said the same for a Muslim contender. And another survey indicated that Americans rate atheists below Muslims, recent immigrants, homosexuals and other groups as "sharing their vision of American society." Moreover, in the words of the late Jerry Falwell—who once said that God is pro-war—"If you're not a born-again Christian, you're a failure as a human being." We salute, then, a few *successful* human beings:

- The individual who placed the winning bid of $1,800 on eBay for a slab of concrete with a smudge of driveway sealant resembling the face of Jesus.
- The man who tried to crucify himself after seeing "pictures of God on the computer." He took two pieces of wood, nailed them together in the form of a cross and placed it on his living-room floor. He proceeded to hammer one of his hands to the crucifix, using a 14-penny nail. According to a county sheriff spokesperson, "When he realized that he was unable to nail his other hand to the board, he called 911." It was unclear whether he was seeking assistance for his injury or help in nailing his other hand down.
- The Sunday School teacher who advised one of his students to write on his penis, "What would Jesus do?" Presumably, "Jerk off" was not considered to be the correct answer.

It was a pleasant surprise when Barack Obama acknowledged "nonbelievers" in his inauguration speech. However, I don't exempt my fellow atheists from criticism. I view as foolish those believers and skeptics alike who are waging a battle against the teaching of meditation in publicly funded schools, as though slow, deep breathing is necessarily and automatically a religious practice. What's next, forbidding the teaching of empathy because that's what Christians and Jews are supposed to practice?

Similarly, I ridicule China's atheist leaders for banning Tibet's living Buddhas from reincarnation without permission. According to the order, issued by the State Administration for Religious Affairs, "The so-called reincarnated living Buddha without government approval is illegal and invalid." The regulation is aimed at limiting the influence of the Dalai Lama, even though China officially *denies* the possibiity of reincarnation. (I used to believe in reincarnation, but that was in a previous lifetime.)

China is a Big-Brother, slave-labor-driven, human-rights-violating, Maoist dictatorship, from which the United States government borrows trillions, then proceeds to purchase "Made in China" American flags, poisoned food and leadened toys. America remains a living paradox, where we are force-fed deceit and misinformation so that the government can continue to fund inhumane and illegal activities—yet we live in a country where at least we still have the freedom to openly condemn the government and the corporations that continue enabling each other to new levels of corruption and inhumanity. I'm truly grateful for that.

"Thank you, God."

"*SHUT UP, YOU SUPERSTITIOUS FOOL!*"

GREAT MOMENTS IN MEMORY LOSS

On *Meet the Press* in August 2007, *Time* magazine's Matt Cooper stated: "Karl Rove told me about Valerie Plame's identity on July 11, 2003. I called him because Ambassador Wilson was in the news that week. I didn't know Ambassador Wilson even had a wife until I talked to Karl Rove and he said that she worked at the agency and she worked on WMD. I mean, to imply that he didn't know about it or that this was all a leak by someone else, or he heard it as some rumor out in the hallway, is nonsense."

Which explains why Scooter Libby, the man with a steel-trap mind, underwent one of those under-oath memory losses concerning Rove's role in outing Plame, just as former Attorney General Alberto Gonzales couldn't recall his own role in the politically motivated firing of several local U.S. attorneys. During the Bush years, there was so much covering of asses that Washington started to look like a Christo art project.

What was it again that Condoleezza Rice testified she couldn't remember telling George Bush? Something about sleeper cells in the United States? Or was it stem cells? Does any reasonable person believe that she really forgot? If she didn't tell Bush, she was covering her own ass. If she did tell him and he did nothing, she was covering *his* ass. Maybe the 9/11 Commision should've offered her HT-0712, the "Mind Viagra" pill that restores memory in fruit flies and mice. But would that make any difference if she was consciously resorting to blatant deception in the guise of false memory-loss syndrome?

In Bob Woodward's book, *Plan of Attack*, his on-the-record interviews instigated a couple of juicy ass-covering lies.

Item: Donald Rumsfeld (who, according to Dick Cheney, has "near perfect recall") said—referring to the impending attack on Iraq—that he didn't remember assuring Saudi Ambassador Prince Bandar, "You can take that to the bank." Then Woodward produced a transcript of the taped interview, and there it was.

Item: The *New York Times* reported that "Secretary of State Colin Powell disputed Woodward's account. . . . He said that he had an excellent relationship with Vice President Dick Cheney, and that he did not recall referring to officials at the Pentagon loyal to Cheney as the 'Gestapo office.'" Who among us would be unable to recall uttering such an epithet? In fact, Powell later apologized for it.

Robert Draper's biography of George Bush, *Dead Certain*, published in September 2007, reveals a significant lapse in Bush's memory. He couldn't recall his disastrous decision, two months after the U.S. invasion of Iraq in March 2003, to disband the Iraqi army, which alienated former soldiers and drove many into anti-American militant groups.

"The policy was to keep the army intact," Bush said. "Didn't happen."

Then why, Draper wanted to know, did his chief administrator for Iraq, L. Paul Bremer, issue an order to dissolve the 400,000-person army without pay? After all, the policy was based on information provided by the CIA that the army would remain intact.

"Yeah, I can't remember," Bush responded. "I'm sure I said, 'This is the policy'—what happened?"

When Ronald Reagan testified before the committee investigating the Iran/Contra scandal, he was unable to recall whether he had approved trading weapons for hostages, testifying 130 times, "I don't remember." During his 1980 campaign, there had been rumblings of senility, and Reagan publicly offered to take a senility test if the proper authorities concluded that he had become senile, but nobody ever took him up on it. Perhaps his convenient losses of memory were actually early tremors of the Alzheimer's disease that plagued him for the last ten years of his life.

Nowadays, there are other excuses. A reader wrote to the medical advice column, "People's Pharmacy" by Joe and Teresa Graedon, in the *Los Angeles Times*:

"I took Lipitor for more than a year, and I thought I was doing great. My cholesterol levels dropped significantly with no side effects. Then I began having problems remembering names. Sometimes it took me till noon to gather my scattered thoughts enough to work. I couldn't put a complete sentence together, and I began avoiding situations that required meeting with people. I'm in the advertising and marketing business, but I avoided clients and preferred to work by e-mail. After reading one of your articles that linked Lipitor to memory problems, I immediately contacted my doctor, and he agreed to a holiday from Lipitor. It took a few months, but my memory has returned. Memory problems should be listed as a side effect of Lipitor."

And the answer: "Amnesia is listed as an infrequent side effect of Lipitor, and memory loss is noted as a potential side effect of other cholesterol-lowering drugs such as Lescol, Mevacor, Pravachol and Zocor. Although this seems to be rare, we have heard from readers who have had difficulty with names, numbers and concentration while taking one of these. Some have even reported episodes in which they could not remember their address, spouse or occupation."

But how to account for the epidemic of memory loss among Bush administration officials?

In May 2004, *Newsweek* stated that a memo written by White House counsel Alberto Gonzales after the September 11 attacks may have established the legal foundation that allowed for the abusive treatment of Iraqi prisoners. *Newsweek* reported that in January 2002, Gonzales wrote to President Bush that, in his judgment, the post-9/11 security environment "renders obsolete [the Geneva Convention's] strict limitations on questioning of enemy prisoners and renders quaint some of its provisions." Quaint! According to *Newsweek*, Colin Powell "hit the roof" when he read the memo, and he fired off his own note to Bush, warning that the new rules "will reverse over a century of U.S. policy and practice" and have "a high cost in terms of negative international reaction." But then, on *Meet the Press*, he claimed that he did not recall the Gonzales memo. Huh?

There's an explanation, though. In November 2003, Powell was interviewed in Washington by Abdul Rahman Al-Rashed, correspondent for a London-based Saudi newspaper. Referring to Powell's description of his international killer-schedule, Al-Rashad asked, "So do you use sleeping tablets to organize yourself?"

"Yes," Powell replied. "Well, I wouldn't call them that. They're a wonderful medication. How would you call it? They're called Ambien, which is very good. You don't use Ambien? Everybody here uses Ambien."

So I decided to check out the side effects of Ambien: "Sleep medicines may cause the special type of memory loss known as amnesia. When this occurs, a person may not remember what has happened for several hours after taking the medicine. This is usually not a problem, since most people fall asleep after taking the medicine. Memory loss can be a problem, however, when sleep medicines are taken while traveling, such as during an airplane flight, and the person wakes up before the effect of the medicine is gone. This has been called 'traveler's amnesia.' Memory problems are not common while taking Ambien. In most instances memory problems can be avoided if you take Ambien only when you are able to get a full night's sleep (7 to 8 hours) before you need to be active again. Be sure to talk to your doctor if you think you are having memory problems."

If you remember to talk to your doctor, that is.

In May 2004, an issue of *Neuron* confirmed previous models of memory recall that found sensory-specific components of a memory are preserved in sensory-related areas of the brain. The hippocampus can draw on this stored sensory information to create vivid recall. Which is why, even after you've returned from a vacation, you may still fully recall the sights, sounds, tastes and smells of some of its particularly memorable moments. For their study, the researchers mapped brain activity in human volunteers who sampled different odors and viewed pictures of various objects.

Speaking of different odors, during the 2007 Republican primaries, Fred Thompson claimed that he doesn't remember much about the 2005 Terri Schiavo controversy concerning whether the severely brain-damaged woman's husband had the right to remove her feeding tube after she had spent fifteen years as an unconscious political football. "I can't pass judgment on it," Thompson said. "That's going back in history. I don't remember the details of it," even though in the summer of that same year he discussed that case with John Roberts when he helped prep him for his Supreme Court confirmation hearings, and in November he appeared in a *Law & Order* episode about a husband trying to disconnect his wife's feeding tube over her family's objections. Rudy Giuliani also pleaded a faulty memory when a reporter asked him if he had supported the efforts to keep Schiavo alive. "I believe I did," he replied. "It's a while ago—I am not sure now."

In April 2009, former CIA director Porter Goss wrote in an op-ed piece in the *Washington Post* that he was "slack-jawed to read that members [of Congress] claim to have not understood that the techniques on which they were briefed were to actually be employed; or that specific techniques such as 'waterboarding' were never mentioned." He labeled these claims "a disturbing epidemic of amnesia." But House Speaker Nancy Pelosi managed to remember that "The CIA was misleading the Congress" and that "The only mention of waterboarding at that briefing was that it was not being employed."

This was another case of Bill Clinton's infamous rationale, "It depends on what the meaning of 'is' is." Here, it was the CIA briefing Congress in September 2002 that "We are not using waterboarding," knowing that the truth was "We *have been* using waterboarding." And the irony is that such torture, ostensibly to extract truth from accused terrorists, was actually used to extract *lies* from them in order to lend support to the Bush administration's lies about the non-existent relationship between Saddam Hussein and Al Qaida.

As for short-term memory loss, Wes Nisker writes in *The Big Bang, the Buddha, and the Baby Boom: The Spiritual Experiments of My Generation*:

"Recent research in molecular biology has given us a clue to the connection between THC, the psychoactive ingredient in marijuana, and the actual experience of getting high. It turns out that our body produces its own version of THC and that the human brain and nervous system have a whole network of receptors for this cannabinoid-like substance. That means you've got a stash inside of you right now, and nobody can even bust you for it. Our body's natural THC was discovered by Israeli neuro-scientists, who named it anandamide, from the Sanskrit word for 'inner bliss.'

"The scientists believe that our system produces this

THC equivalent to aid in pain relief, for mild sedation, and also to help us forget. It is very important that we forget, because if we remembered everything that registers our senses from moment to moment, we would be flooded with memory and could not function. So anandamide helps us edit the input of the world by blocking or weakening our synaptic pathways, our memory lanes."

The next time somebody reminds you, "Don't bogart that joint," at least you'll have a scientific explanation, if you can only remember what it is.

TRASHING THE RIGHT TO READ

Before Kenneth Foster's death sentence was revoked at the last minute in August 2007, he had read a book, *Welcome to the Terrordome*, and he wrote a letter to the author, Dave Zirin:

"I have never had the opportunity to view sports in this way. And as I went through these revelations I began to have epiphanies about the way sports have a similar existence in prison. The similarities shook me. Facing execution, the only thing that I began to get obsessive about was how to get heard and be free, and as the saying goes, you can't serve two gods. Sports, as you know, becomes a way of life. You monitor it, you almost come to breathe it. Sports becomes a way of life in prison, because it becomes a way of survival. For men that don't have family or friends to help them financially, it becomes a way to occupy your time. That's another sad story in itself, but it's the root to many men's obsession with sports."

Zirin writes, "It didn't matter if he was on death row or Park Avenue, I felt smarter having read his words. But even more satisfying was the thought that thinking about sports took his mind—for a moment—away from his imminent death, the 11-year-old daughter he will never touch and the words he will never write. I thought sending him my first book, *What's My Name Fool? Sports and Resistance in the U.S.*, would be a good follow-up."

But a form titled "Texas Dept. of Criminal Justice, Publication Review/Denial Notification" stated that this book about sports history was banned from Death Row because "It contains material that a reasonable person would construe as written solely for the purpose of communicating information designed to achieve the breakdown of prisons through offender disruption such as strikes or riots." Two pages were specifically mentioned.

Page 44 includes a quote from Jackie Robinson's autobiography referring to the blatant racism he suffered early in his rookie season: "I felt tortured and I tried to just play ball and ignore the insults but it was really getting to me. For one wild and rage-crazed moment I thought, 'To hell with Mr. Rickey's noble experiment. To hell with the image of the patient black freak I was supposed to create.' I could throw down my bat, stride over to that Phillies dugout, grab one of those white sons of bitches, and smash his teeth in with my despised black fist. Then I could walk away from it all."

And page 55 includes a passage about Jack Johnson's defeat of the "Great White Hope," Jim Jeffries: "Johnson was faster, stronger and smarter than Jeffries. He knocked Jeffries out with ease. After Johnson's victory, there were race riots around the country in Illinois, Missouri, New York, Ohio, Pennsylvania, Colorado, Texas and Washington, D.C. Most of the riots consisted of white lynch mobs attacking blacks, and blacks fighting back. This reaction to a boxing match was one of the most widespread racial uprisings in the U.S. until the 1968 assassination of civil rights leader Dr. Martin Luther King Jr."

Zirin points out that "There was a time in Texas when it was illegal to teach slaves to read. The fear was that ideas could turn anger often directed inward into action against those with their boots on black necks. It is perhaps the most fitting possible tribute to Jackie Robinson and Jack Johnson that they still strike fear into the hearts of those wearing the boots."

In the Dallas County jail, one of the largest in the country, *all* publications are refused, including daily newspapers such as the *Dallas Morning News*. "They seem to have a rather callous disregard for the Constitution," said Paul Wright, publisher of Seattle-based *Prison Legal News*, with a circulation of 6,000. He filed a federal lawsuit challenging the ban on First Amendment grounds, and won. His lawyer, Scott Medlock, prisoner rights attorney with the Texas Civil Rights Project, points out that some jails have argued that prisoners can watch TV news in jail, so they don't need access to publications.

Prison Legal News is also preparing a lawsuit against the Utah Department of Corrections for a policy that bars all books except those that are shipped directly from Barnes & Noble. Generally, prisons require that books be sent directly from the publisher or a major distributor, for security reasons. Otherwise, a spokesperson for one jail explains, "There's a possibility something could be in one of the pages that we don't want. There could be little bits of drugs in the pages."

"We have not yet sued them." Wright told me, "since

they only sporadically censor us and aren't letting us develop a good fact pattern."

A spokesperson for the Los Angeles County Sheriff's Department said that its jails allow inmates to receive books from booksellers after checking to see whether they can be fashioned into a weapon, promote violence or have sexually explicit content. Across the country, only paperbacks are accepted. Hardcovers are rejected because they provide "source material" for fashioning weapons. When the Supreme Court ruled that law libraries did not have to be provided to prisoners, jails in Montana not only removed the entire contents of the law library, but they also removed the typewriters.

Washington State has tried to keep *Prison Legal News* itself out of prisons. First, the Department of Corrections prohibited inmates from receiving nonprofits. *PLN* sued and won. Next, the state issued a rule that inmates couldn't receive publications that were paid out of their trust accounts. *PLN* managed to get that rule overturned too. Then the prisons adopted a policy of not delivering subscription-renewal notices. *PLN* took that to court and succeeded in getting the policy reversed. *PLN* has won similar lawsuits or settlements in Alabama, California, Michigan, Nevada and Oregon.

While serving five years in a California prison for growing medical marijuana, Todd McCormick contributed a couple of stories—about his experiences with psilocybin and ketamine—to my collection, *Magic Mushrooms and Other Highs: From Toad Slime to Ecstasy*, and when it was published, I immediately sent him a copy. But the warden rejected it "because on pages 259–261, it describes the process of squeezing toads to obtain illicit substances which could be detrimental to the security, good order and discipline of the institution."

This was pure theater of cruelty. Federal correctional facilities do not have a toad problem, and outside accomplices have not been catapulting loads of toads over barbed wire fences to provide the fuel for a prison riot.

McCormick wrote to me, "Can you believe this shit! I wonder how much we pay the guy/girl who actually sits and reads every book that comes in for offending passages. How about you tear out pages 259-261 and re-send this book back with a copy of the rejection and a notation that the offending pages have been removed."

Which is exactly what I did. This time, though, my cover letter to the warden was ignored, and the book was returned, stamped *Unauthorized*. I had called their bluff. Obviously, McCormick was being punished simply because he could be. I then corresponded with several friends in prisons around the country to find out what inmates had not been allowed to read. I wanted to see other examples of arbitrary and frivolous censorship by prison personnel. Here are some results of my informal survey:

- "The Texas Department of Corrections blocked Bo Lozoff's *Breaking Out of Jail*, a book about teaching meditation to prison inmates."
- "Disallowed: *Trainspotting* because of its 'glorification of drug use.' Tom Robbins' *Still Life With Woodpecker* because it has a chapter that 'contains information about bombmaking.'"
- "An inmate couldn't get nude pictures of his wife sent to him but he could get a subscription to *Playboy*. The rationale: A wife deserved more respect."

- "They kept out *The Anarchists Cookbook*. And no kiddie porn, no tales or photos suggesting sex with a guard, no photos showing frontal or rear nudity—not even a wife or friend."
- "The Utah prison system banned *Rolling Stone* as being an anarchist publication."
- "*A Revolution in Kindness* is banned from the Louisiana State Penitentiary at Angola as 'a threat to internal security.' It was intended for Herman Wallace, who contributed an essay about how he organized a chess tournament on his cell block as a way of easing tensions and minimizing violence between inmates. Wallace is one of the Angola Three—Black Panthers who have been in solitary confinement for [more than three decades] trying to improve conditions in the 'bloodiest prison in America' in the early 1970s."
- "All hardback books forbidden, because the covers could be fashioned into weapons. Educational textbooks—a new rule precludes prisoners on Death Row [including this particular prisoner] or in lockdown from taking correspondence courses—and I've had a couple of books returned to sender on the claim they appeared to be for a course. *MAPS* [Multidisciplinary Association for Psychedelic Studies]—their publication was sent back several times because maps are not allowed in here. *High Times* was repeatedly denied because it posed a danger to the safe, secure and orderly operation of the institution. 'Smut mags' like *Hustler* are reviewed monthly."
- "There's a whole new genre of men's magazines—*Maxim*, *Stuff*, *For Him*—which show it all except for nipples and beaver. Now the feds want to ban *Maxim* due to 'security' reasons. The 'rejected mail' slip they send you

when some verboten material arrives has boxes to check (to specify offending matter), one of which says 'pubic hair.'"

- "Peace activist William Combs spent eight days in solitary confinement for receiving and sharing with other inmates what federal authorities consider disruptive, if not subversive, political literature. The offending 'propaganda' included commentary by such extremists as Bill Moyers and Ellen Goodman, and included an article published in *Reader's Digest*. The common thread was that they all questioned the wisdom of government policy."

The name of the game is control in the guise of security—a microcosm of the nation outside prison walls—the practice of power without compassion.

After *Magic Mushrooms and Other Highs* was rejected for the second time, I appealed to the Regional Director of the Bureau of Prisons (as instructed by the warden) for an independent review. I also wrote to the ACLU. I heard back from neither.

Todd McCormick was released from prison in December 2003. Among so many other things to catch up on, he would finally be able to read what he had written. However, he was discharged to a halfway house, where all his books and magazines were confiscated as "paraphernalia."

THE THOUGHT POLICE AT WORK

Paul Revere is remembered for riding his horse through the streets of pre-revolutionary America and shouting, "The British are coming! The British are coming!" These days, a contemporary version of Paul Revere would be riding his Harley-Davidson through the streets of pre-revolutionary America and shouting at the top of his lungs, "The thought police are coming! The thought police are coming!"

A shocking violation of the First Amendment was foisted upon Ed Forchion, also known as the New Jersey Weedman. He had been sentenced to ten years in prison after pleading guilty to possessing twenty-five pounds of marijuana. He served more than sixteen months behind bars before being paroled on an early release program, and then he was arrested again for violating his parole.

But what had he done wrong? He committed the heinous "crime" of advocating the reform of marijuana laws. It's that simple, and it's that terrifying. Forchion had the audacity to exercise his right to free speech by filming several public service announcements that expressed his point of view. The injustice is intensified by the fact that those commercials were never aired.

Forchion is a Rastafarian who hasn't exactly tried to keep a low profile. He's run for Congress three times and smoked pot on the floor of the state Assembly as an act of civil disobedience. But now he had become a political prisoner—put behind bars *for his ideas*. U.S. District Judge Joseph Irenas scheduled a hearing where state officials had to show cause for imprisoning him. The judge pointed out that Forchion probably would not have been returned to prison if he had not spoken publicly about the drug laws.

Forchion had already served six months. Now, Irenas ordered his release, stating that "speaking to the press, protesting and handing out pamphlets outside of the courthouse, running a Web site, or producing and appearing in television commercials [are] clearly protected by the First

Amendment, particularly since [this behavior] primarily involved [Forchion's] belief that marijuana should be legalized."

But wait. Because the judge ruled that Forchion should be returned to the early release program, he *also* ordered that Forchion cannot promote the illegal use of marijuana once he is released. And there's more. Although his commercials dealt with First Amendment issues and the war on drugs, they did not explicitly advocate the use of marijuana.

Former White House press secretary Ari Fleischer once chastised Bill Maher for speaking out against the American invasion and occupation of Iraq with these words: "He should watch what he says." Now that warning has developed tentacles. One such extension would be: "You better watch what you *wear*."

Item: Shana Weiss wanted to share a nostalgic moment with her family and friends. "I responded to those ads we see each night," she explains, "sandwiched between iPod promos and Tiffany settings touting the virtues of PhotoStamps." She ordered two sets of stamps—"one set of my 5-year-old in his Happy Feet ski hat, and one set of my 8-year-old in his T-shirt that reads *Make Cupcakes Not War*"—but when the package arrived, the latter set was missing. A customer service flunky told her, "Your order has been rejected because it does not meet our content guidelines."

Item: Ten-year-old Lydia Smith and her mother were taking a lunch break while shopping for new church clothes at the Battlefield Mall in Springfield, Missouri, when Lydia was approached by a security guard who asked her to remove the bandanna she was wearing. He handed a copy of the Battlefield Mall Code to her mom. Among a list of seventeen possible offenses, Lydia had violated the one that reads: "Failing to be fully clothed or wearing apparel which is likely to provide a disturbance or embroil other groups or the general public in open conflict." Her threatening bandanna was decorated with flowers, smiley faces and peace signs.

Les Morris, a spokesperson for Simon Property Group—which invokes similar rules at their 285 properties in thirty-nine states and Puerto Rico—explained that the mall's primary responsibility is to protect its customers, tenants and employers. Ironically, at least one retail store at the Battlefield Mall, namely J.C. Penney, *sells* those forbidden bandannas. Morris reasoned, "There are things we sell that it's okay to own them, but to use them in the mall setting is inappropriate."

Item: One afternoon, Mike Ferner, who served as a Navy corpsman during the Vietnam War, was sitting and drinking a cup of iced coffee at the Veterans Administration Medical Center in Chicago when a V.A. cop walked up to him and said, "Okay, you've had your fifteen minutes, it's time to go. You can't be in here protesting," said Officer Adkins, pointing to Ferner's *Veterans for Peace* T-shirt.

"Well, I'm not protesting, I'm having a cup of coffee."

"No, not with that shirt. You're protesting and you have to go."

"Not before I finish my coffee." The cop insisted that he leave. "Hey, listen," Ferner said, "I'm a veteran. This is a V.A. facility. I'm sitting here not talking to anybody, having a cup of coffee. I'm not protesting, and you can't kick me out."

"You'll either go or we'll arrest you."

"Well, you'll just have to arrest me."

Ferner was handcuffed and led away to the facility's security office, read his rights, searched and written up. He was charged with disorderly conduct. Charges of criminal trespass and weapons possession were dismissed, but he was informed that his weapon—a Swiss Army knife with a bottle opener, a tweezers and a reusable toothpick—would have to be destroyed. I asked if he would be wearing "that shirt," the one that says *Veterans for Peace* with their logo— a military helmet and a dove—to court.

"You betcha," he replied.

Then there was Richard Humphreys, who happened to get into a harmless barroom discussion with a truck driver. A bartender who overheard their conversation realized that George Bush was scheduled to visit Sioux Falls the next day, and he told police that Humphreys—who was actually making a joke with a Biblical reference—had talked about a "burning Bush" and the possibility of someone pouring a flammable liquid on Bush and lighting it. Humphreys was arrested for threatening the president.

"I said God might speak to the world through a burning Bush," he testified during his trial. "I had said that before and I thought it was funny."

Nevertheless, he was found guilty and sentenced to more than three years in prison. He decided to appeal, on the basis that his comment was a prophecy, protected under his right to freedom of speech. America continues to embrace suppresion in the guise of security. And in that process, rampant paranoia has now become our Gross National Product.

In May 2007, the Pentagon announced that it was cutting off service members' access to YouTube, MySpace and eleven other Web sites, some of which are used by soldiers on the front lines of Iraq and Afghanistan to post videos for friends and family back home. A few days earlier, the military had launched its own channel on YouTube, offering a "boots on the ground" perspective of combat scenes. That same month, an Iraqi government policy banned news photographers and camera operators from filming bombing scenes, so that video shot by citizens and uploaded to YouTube could become the *only* imagery that the public sees of such devastation.

Finally, we come to the case of Brian Dalton. When he was 22 and living in Columbus, Ohio, he was on probation after having served time in prison. He had been convicted a few years previously for possessing pornographic photos of children. After being released, he kept a private journal in which he wrote down his fantasies about the sexual abuse and torture of fictional children. He made up their names.

He had simply been exorcising his own demons. He never showed his journal to anyone else. But then one day it was found during a search of his home by his probation officer. There were fourteen pages of imaginary encounters with three children, age 10 and 11, who were kept caged in a basement.

Dalton was arrested and charged under an Ohio law that prohibits the creation of obscene material involving minors. The prosecutor insisted that the statute covered not only images of real children, but also printed or written words involving fictional children, including words that had been intended for the eyes *only of the writer himself.*

However, members of the grand jury found those stories so offensive that they asked the detective, who was reading them out loud, to stop almost as soon as he began. For whatever reason, fear or foolishness, Dalton pleaded guilty instead of challenging his conviction, and he was sentenced to seven years in prison plus eighteen months for violation of his probation. Thus he became the first person ever convicted in the United States for child pornography that involved writings rather than photographs, films or other images of real children. Nor had he ever disseminated those writings. The fact that he would actually go to prison for what he had fantasized in his own personal diary is way more shocking than any words that he wrote in it.

Although Dalton later asked to withdraw his guilty plea in order to fight the constitutionality of the law, that request was turned down by a judge. The ACLU appealed his decision, but an appeals court threw out Dalton's guilty plea. This form of persecution had its own history.

In 1969, in a case being appealed from Georgia, the Supreme Court ruled that, "Given the present state of knowledge, the state may no more prohibit mere possession of obscene matter on the ground that it may lead to antisocial conduct than it may prohibit possession of chemistry books on the ground that they may lead to the manufacture of homemade spirits."

The court asserted that an American has a constitutional right "to read or observe what he pleases—the right to satisfy his intellectual and emotional needs in the privacy of his own home, and the right to be free from state inquiry into the contents of his library. If the First Amendment means anything, it means that a state has no business telling a man, sitting alone in his own house, what books he may read or films he may watch."

However, in a 1990 case arising from Ohio, the Supreme Court in effect reversed itself, holding that the mere possession of child pornography could be prohibited, based on the state's "compelling interests in protecting the physical and psychological well-being of minors and in destroying the market for the exploitative use of children by penalizing those who possess and view the offending materials."

Here's how the court justified that ruling: "Evidence suggests that pedophiles use child pornography to seduce other children into sexual activity." Obviously, none of this applied to Brian Dalton, but that was irrelevant to the new breed of thought police. They're becoming more and more out of control.

Some elementary schools have even gone so far as to ban parents from bringing cameras to record their children performing in the annual Christmas pageant, because authorities are afraid that those videotapes might somehow make their way into the horny hands of pedophiles.

DONUTS, COFFEE AND WEED

The irony of the Silly Season in America is that those who contribute to it seem to lack a sense of humor. Here are a couple of cases in point.

The folks at Dunkin' Donuts figured they had made a smart move when they hired Rachael Ray—the host of *30 Minute Meals* on the Food Network plus her own syndicated daytime talk show—to hold a cup of iced coffee in their TV commercials and online ads. Simple enough idea, right?

But a conservative Web site, *Little Green Footballs*,

compared the fringed black-and-white scarf Ray was wearing to those typically worn by Muslim extremists.

Next came right-wing blogger Michelle Malkin, asserting that the scarf did in fact resemble a *keffiyeh*, which, Malkin wrote, "has come to symbolize murderous Palestinian jihad. Popularized by Yasser Arafat and a regular adornment of Muslim terrorists appearing in beheading and hostage-taking videos, the apparel has been mainstreamed by both ignorant (and not-so-ignorant) fashion designers, celebrities, and left-wing icons."

Suddenly Dunkin' Donuts was bombarded with so many calls from reporters seeking a comment that they chickened out and decided to pull the ad, explaining that "the possibility of misperception detracted from its original intention to promote our iced coffee." Laughter had been replaced by fear.

Now everybody wanted to get in the act. A YouTube video titled *Rachael Ray Is a Terrorist* made fun of the controversy, complete with a narrator admitting, "Yes, because when I look at Rachael Ray, I think 9/11."

And on MSNBC's nightly news show, *Countdown*, Keith Olbermann labeled Dunkin' Donuts as the "Worst Person in the World." He said, "They were as weak as their decaf," and called for public punishment of the chain. "How about this? How about the rest of us boycott Dunkin' Donuts for giving in to fascists like Michelle Malkin? And for giving weight to perhaps the most absurd idea the lunatic fringers have ever belched forth—that there are terrorist scarves. Terrorist scarves! Dunkin' Donuts—time to stop buying the donuts."

Rachael Ray will soon present her new recipe for Al Qaediced Coffee.

The other example of severe silliness concerns a town in California called Weed—population, 3,000—named after Abner Weed, who was a state senator a century ago. A small brewery there has been placing a slogan, *Try Legal Weed*, on the bottle caps of its beer. Just a harmless joke, right?

Not to the tunnel vision of the U.S. Treasury Department's Alcohol and Tobacco Tax and Trade Bureau. They perceive those three little words to be an invitation to smoke marijuana. So they sent a warning to Vaune Dillmann, the 61-year-old owner of the Mt. Shasta Brewing Company. If he didn't cease and desist, he could be risking fines or sanctions. This threat could conceivably ruin his livelihood.

"This is ludicrous, bizarre," said Dillmann, "like meeting Big Brother face to face. Forget freedom of speech and the First Amendment. They are the regulatory gods, a judge and jury all rolled into one. This is a life-or-death issue for my business."

A spokesperson for the agency tried to justify its position: "We consider it to be a drug reference, and find it to be false and misleading to the consumer in terms of what may or may not be the properties contained within that product."

The mayor of Weed complained, "It's just plain goofy to me the federal government is making so much of a fuss over this. I can sort of understand their point, but it all seems a little overboard."

Under the headline "Government Is Keeping Us Safe From Bottle Caps," the *Record Searchlight* editorialized: "Let's get real. Anyone old enough to legally buy a six-pack is mature enough not to be dragged into a life of drug-addled debauchery by a message on the bottle cap."

Gas stations sell T-shirts that say *High on Weed*—the

town is at an elevation of 3,500 feet—and a placard at the town's exit states, *Temporarily Out of Weed*. Dillmann's bottled brews include Shastafarian Porter and Mountain High. His *Try Legal Weed* slogan has already appeared on more than 400,000 beer bottle caps. He recently bought another 400,000, and if they can't be used, he'll be out $10,000.

In August 2008, surrendering to public outrage, that federal bureau reversed itself and approved the bottle cap with that controversial slogan.

"Weed fought the law," Dillmann reacted, "and Weed won!"

But just wait till the government finds out about *This Bud's For You*.

WELCOME TO CAMP MOGUL

My irreverent friend, Khan Manka, Chairman & CEO of Manka Brothers Studios, had broken his ankle and was afraid he wouldn't be able to attend the twenty-sixth annual gathering of the nation's most powerful executives and their trophy wives in Sun Valley, Idaho. I really wanted to spy on this 2008 summer camp for billionaires, so I suggested that Manka get a wheelchair; then I could serve as his official wheelchair pusher. He immediately went for the idea.

This by-now traditional five-day extravaganza for 300 guests was hosted by Wall Street investment banker Herbert Allen, president and CEO of Allen & Company. There were moguls all over the campground, overflowing with the country's most influential leaders in business, entertainment and media. I could feel myself developing a severe case of imposter syndrome.

Saturday was Talent Night, and it was absolutely hysterical. Part-time Sun Valley resident Tom Hanks served as the emcee. Warren Buffett was the opening act, performing a medley of Jimmy Buffett songs, all rendered out of tune. *Amazon.com* founder Jeff Bezos skillfully juggled five Kindles (wireless electronic books). Edgar Bronfman from Warner Music—dressed like the character Tevye in *Fiddler on the Roof*—sang with zest, "If I Were a Rich Man." Yahoo CEO Jerry Yang—who had previously turned down an offer from Microsoft to buy Yahoo—sang a duet with the ex-CEO of Microsoft, Bill Gates, harmonizing on a song from *Annie Get Your Gun*, "Anything You Can Do, I Can Do Better." Meg Whitman of eBay did a striptease, auctioning off each item of clothing, one at a time, and over 3 million dollars was raised for an unnamed charity. Oracle Corp. CEO Larry Ellison gave a hilarious lecture on "How to Destroy Evidence and Make False Statements."

There had been a lot of drinking in the evening, and it was obviously too much booze that loosened up Fox mogul Rupert Murdoch's tongue. He was shouting at the moon: "Who says there are 27 million slaves around the world? And where the fuck can *I* get one? How would anybody know it's 27 million anyway? Do they have census takers or *what*? You tell me! I'll decide!"

Also, a screaming match broke out between Google co-founder Sergei Brin and Google CEO Eric Schmidt over that infamous cover of the *New Yorker* that depicted Barack and Michelle Obama as the new president and first lady, a terrorist couple doing that fist-bump gesture in the Oval Office. Sergei thought it was a brilliant satirical illustration, but Eric thought it was racist and irresponsible.

The previous year, 2007, the surprise guest was former British Prime Minister Tony Blair. Now it was Steven Beschloss, the editor of a new magazine, scheduled to be launched in October 2008 and delivered to 100,000 U.S. households with an average net worth of $25 million. There were piles of preview copies scattered about.

While Beschloss was holding court in an outdoor area, annoying mosquitoes kept buzzing around the crowd. Mark Zuckerberg, the founder of Facebook, yelled at him, "I guess we'll never hear *your* readers whining about a mental recession. And those of your subscribers who were in the subprime mortgage industry—these mosquitoes are *their* fault, because, along with all the home foreclosures they're responsible for, the stagnant water in abandoned pools turns into new breeding grounds for mosquitoes."

Someone yelled out, "Where are you from, 'In-Your-Facebook?'" Others drowned out Zuckerberg's apparently serious rant by singing the mogul version of a couple of good old-fashioned camp songs, "This Land Is *My* Land, This Land Is *My* Land" and "KumBuyYahoo." I couldn't help but notice that billionaire activist Carl Icahn snapped his fingers as if having an epiphany; a week later he ended up on Yahoo's board of directors.

Khan Manka explained that at these events so-called "informal" meetings between bigwigs always take place where a pair of individuals can have their discussions alone without any interruption—on the golf course, hiking along an isolated trail, fly-fishing at Silver Creek—but Manka had been privy to only one specific example that he could share.

"Back in 1995," he told me, "Disney honcho Michael Eisner met with Robert Iger, who was then the head of ABC. And exactly one month later, these two giant companies merged into one media megamonster. Coincidence? I don't think so. Their deal had been sealed when Eisner and Iger exchanged friendship bracelets that they had worked on at Camp Mogul."

CAMPAIGN IN THE ASS

The Denver Police Department is facing several lawsuits over confrontations with protesters at the Democratic National Convention. The officers had conducted mass arrests and detentions of 154 individuals before and during the convention. One cop, for example, was videotaped pushing a woman to the ground with his baton as he yelled, "Back up, bitch!" The police are being charged with systematically condoning violence against antiwar demonstrators.

Now, a commemorative T-shirt created and distributed by their union, the Denver Police Protective Association, could be offered as evidence of the cops' state of mind. The T-shirt features a menacing depiction of a gigantic, nightstick-wielding cop with a malevolent grin, towering over Denver's downtown skyline and boasting, "We Get Up Early, to BEAT the Crowds," along with the slogan, "2008 DNC." The cop's hat has the image of number 68 inside a circle with a slash going through it, an obvious reference to *Re-create 68*, a protest group that staged several demonstrations.

Shirt producer Nick Rogers said that each of the 1,400 Denver officers was given a free T-shirt, and that they're being sold for $10. He said that the police union predicts sales of about 2,000 shirts. Rogers stated that he hadn't received any complaints about the shirt. But Glenn Spagnuolo, co-founder of *Re-create 68*, did in fact complain that "the members of Denver's police union clearly have no respect for the rights guaranteed by the United States Constitution."

Re-create 68 has demanded an investigation by officials, including the mayor and the safety manager. Spagnuolo says that "The people of Denver were assured by the city that it would respect First Amendment rights during the convention, and that the police officers were being trained to do so. The actions of police during the convention, which involved numerous violations of people's right to freedom of speech and assembly, put the lie to those promises. And now this appalling, tasteless T-shirt shows why."

The Denver Police Department Operations Manual includes a Law Enforcement Code of Ethics, which begins, "As a Law Enforcement Officer, my fundamental duty is to serve mankind, to safeguard lives and property, to protect the innocent against deception, the weak against oppression or intimidation, and the peaceful against violence or disorder; and to respect the Constitutional rights of all men to liberty equality and justice."

Aside from the sexist wording in that opening credo, the T-shirt makes a mockery of the mission statement. Spagnuolo insists that members of his group saw those shirts *before* the convention, and that they reflect the brutality exhibited by Denver police officers during the convention. "We feel like police should not be celebrating violating people's rights," he says. "These shirts set the tone for the beating that our members took."

Martin Vigil, president of the Denver Police Protective Association, insists, "Nothing really happened. It wasn't the event that the antigovernment groups anticipated, and the T-shirts are a satirical comment on that, given to officers after the event as a 'thank you' for a perfect convention." The police group contends, "Those activists just don't get the joke."

"Count us among those who don't find it very funny," stated a *Denver Post* editorial. "The T-shirt was supposedly a joke. 'We get up early to beat the crowds.' Get it? 'Beat' the crowds. The shirt undermines the efforts the Denver Police Department has made to boost its credibility in the community. . . . Denver police leadership has been working hard in recent years to improve both its use-of-force practices and its image within the community after several controversial shootings."

In any case, there's a certain meta-irony about the name *Re-create 68*. Not only did the crossed-out 68 on the hat of the cop on the T-shirt refer to *Re-create 68*, but *Re-create 68* itself was a reference to the 1968 Democratic convention in Chicago where protesters were severely beaten by police.

Moreover, at the 1996 Democratic convention in Chicago, there were T-shirts with the logo of the Chicago Police Department and the legend, "Democratic National Convenion Chicago—1996—We Kicked Your Father's Ass in 1968—Wait 'Til You See What We Do to You!"

That's the trouble with a police state. The cops think it's a *good* thing.

A friend in Denver during the convention walked past the front steps of the police department in Denver, where a lot of cops were assembled for an outdoor photo. One of them called out, "Whose streets?" The rest of the cops chanted back, "*Our* streets," breaking out in laughter.

Another friend was being hassled by a cop in New York. His young son muttered, "This is a police state."

"It's not a police state," the cop responded. "It's a police world."

BEHIND THE INFAMOUS TWINKIE DEFENSE

November 27, 2008, marked the thirtieth anniversary of the assassination of progressive San Francisco Mayor George Moscone and Supervisor Harvey Milk, who was becoming the gay equivalent of Martin Luther King Jr. Two weeks earlier, the killer, Dan White, had resigned from the Board of Supervisors, but now, having learned the previous night that Moscone would not grant his request to be reappointed, he had decided to seek the ultimate revenge.

Although White, a former cop, confessed shortly after the murders, he would plead not guilty. I was assigned to cover his trial for an alternative weekly, the *San Francisco Bay Guardian*. I'm embarrassed to admit that I said "Thank you" to the sheriff's deputy who frisked me before I could enter the courtroom. However, this was a superfluous ritual, since any journalist who wanted to shoot White was prevented from doing so by wall-to-wall bulletproof glass.

Defense attorney Douglas Schmidt did not want any pro-gay sentiment polluting the verdict, but he wasn't allowed to ask potential jurors if they were gay, so instead he would ask if they had ever supported controversial causes—"like homosexual rights, for instance." One juror came from a family of police—ordinarily, Schmidt would have craved a prospect like him for this jury—but the man mentioned, "I live with a roommate and lover."

Schmidt phrased his next question: "Where does he or she work?"

The answer began, "He"—and the ball game was already over—"works at Holiday Inn."

Throughout the trial, White just sat there as though he had been mainlining epoxy glue. He stared directly ahead, his eyes focused on the crack between two adjacent boxes on the clerk's desk, Olde English type identifying them as "Deft" and "Pltff" for defendant and plaintiff. He didn't testify. Rather, he told his story to several psychiatrists hired by the defense, and *they* repeated those details in court.

At a press conference, Berkeley psychiatrist Lee Coleman denounced the practice of psychiatric testimony, labeling it as "a disguised form of hearsay."

◆ ◆ ◆

The day before the trial began, the assistant district attorney slated to prosecute the case was standing in an elevator at the Hall of Justice. He heard a voice behind him speak his name: "Tom Norman, you're a motherfucker for prosecuting Dan White." He turned around and saw a half-dozen police inspectors. He flushed and faced the door again. These cops were his drinking buddies, but now they were all mad at him.

"I didn't know who said it," he confided to the courtroom artist for a local TV station, "and I didn't want to know."

One could only speculate about the chilling effect that incident had on him, perhaps engendering his sloppy presentation of the prosecution's case. For example, in his opening statement, Norman told the jury that White had reloaded his gun in the mayor's office, but, according to White's confession:

Q: And do you know how many shots you fired [at Moscone]?
A: Uh—no, I don't, I don't, I out of instinct when I, I reloaded the gun, ah—you know, it's just the training I had, you know.

Q: Where did you reload?
A: I reloaded in my office when, when I was—I couldn't out in the hall.

Which made it slightly less instinctive. Norman sought to prove that the murders had been premeditated, yet ignored this evidence of premeditation in White's own confession. If White's reloading of his gun had been, as he said, "out of instinct," then he indeed *would* have reloaded in Moscone's office. And if it were *truly* an instinctive act, then he would have reloaded *again* after killing Milk.

One psychiatrist testified that White must have been mistaken in his recollection of where he reloaded. The evidence on this key question became so muddled that one juror would later recall, "It was a very important issue, but it was never determined where he reloaded—in Moscone's office or just prior to saying, 'Harvey, I want to talk with you.'"

In his confession, White had stated, "I don't know why I put [my gun] on." At the trial, psychiatrists offered reasons ranging from psychological (it was "a security blanket") to practical (for "self-defense" against a People's Temple hit squad; this was a week after the Jonestown massacre). But, as a former police officer and member of the Police Commission told me, "An off-duty cop carrying his gun for protection isn't gonna take extra bullets. If he can't save his life with the bullets already in his gun, then he's done for."

When White's aide, Denise Apcar, picked him up at 10:15 that fateful morning, he didn't come out the front door as he normally would. He emerged from the garage. He had gone down down there to put on his service revolver, a .38 special, which he always kept loaded. He opened a box of extra cartridges, which were packed in rows of five, wrapped ten of them in a handkerchief so they wouldn't rattle, and put them into his pocket.

At one point in the confession to his old friend and former softball coach, Police Inspector Frank Falzon, White claimed, "I was leaving the house to talk, to see the mayor, and I went downstairs to, to make a phone call, and I had my gun there." But there was a phone upstairs, and White was home alone. His wife had already gone to the Hot Potato, a fast-food franchise he had leased. But Falzon didn't question him about that. He neglected to pose a simple question that any kid playing detective would have asked— "Dan, who did you call?"—the answer to which could have been easily verified.

Prosecutor Norman bungled his case and allowed the defense to use White's confession to its own advantage. The mere transcript could never capture the sound of White's anguish. He was like a small boy, sobbing uncontrollably because he wouldn't be allowed to play on the Little League team. When the tape was played in court, some reporters wept, along with members of White's family, spectators, jurors, an assistant D.A.—who had a man-sized tissue box on his table—and Dan White himself, crying both live and on tape simultaneously.

If the prosecution hadn't entered this tape as evidence, the defense could have done so, saving it as the final piece of evidence for dramatic effect. And yet the heart-wrenching confession was contradicted by White's former aide, Apcar. In White's confession, he said that after shooting Moscone, "I was going to go down the stairs, and then I saw Harvey Milk's aide across the hall . . . and then it struck me about what Harvey had tried to do [oppose White's reappointment], and I said, 'Well, I'll go talk to him.'" But Apcar testified that while she was driving White to City Hall, he said he wanted to talk to *both* Moscone and Milk.

White had resigned as supervisor because he couldn't support his wife and baby on a salary of $9,600 a year. He planned to devote himself full time to The Hot Potato, and felt great relief. However, he had been the swing vote, representing downtown real estate interests and the conservative Police Officers Association. With a promise of financial backing, White changed his mind and told Moscone that he wanted his job back.

At first, Moscone said sure, a man has the right to change his mind. But there was opposition to White's return, led by Milk, who had cut off his ponytail and put on a suit but refused to hide his sexual preference. He warned the pragmatic Moscone that giving the homophobic White his seat back would be seen as an anti-gay move in the homosexual community. White had cast the only vote against the gay rights ordinance. But even a mayor who wants to run for reelection has the right to change his mind.

On Sunday evening, November 26, a reporter phoned

White and said, "I can tell you from a very good source in the mayor's office that you definitely are *not* going to be reappointed. Can you comment on that?" "I don't want to talk about it," he replied. "I don't know anything about that." And he hung up.

White stayed on the couch that night, not wanting to keep his wife awake. He didn't get any sleep, just lay there brooding. He decided to go to City Hall on Monday morning.

Now, Mary Ann White sat behind her husband in the front row of spectators, her Madonna-like image in direct view of the jury. Since she was scheduled to testify, prosecutor Norman could have had her excluded from the courtroom. For that matter, he could have excluded from the jury George Mintzer, an executive at the Bechtel Company, which had contributed to White's campaign for supervisor. Mintzer was foreman of the jury.

For Mary Ann, this trial was like a Quaker funeral where mourners share anecdotes about the deceased and you find out things you never knew about someone you'd been living with for years. The day after her own tearful testimony, she was back in the front row, taking notes on the testimony of a psychiatrist who had previously interviewed *her* and taken notes. So now she was writing down poignant squibs of her own recycled observations, such as "Lack of sex drive" and "Danny didn't intend to shoot anyone."

❖ ❖ ❖

J.I. Rodale, health food advocate and publishing magnate, once claimed in an editorial in his magazine, *Prevention*, that Lee Harvey Oswald had been seen holding a Coca-Cola bottle only minutes after the assassination of President John F. Kennedy. He concluded that Oswald was not responsible for the killing because his brain was confused. He was a "sugar drunkard." Rodale, who died of a heart attack during a taping of *The Dick Cavett Show*—in the midst of explaining how good nutrition guarantees a long life—called for a full-scale investigation of crimes caused by sugar consumption.

In a surprise move, Dan White's defense team presented a similar biochemical explanation of *his* behavior, blaming it on compulsive gobbling down of sugar-filled junk-food snacks. This was a purely accidental tactic. Dale Metcalf, a former member of Ken Kesey's Merry Pranksters who had become a lawyer, told me how he happened to be playing chess with Steven Scherr, an associate of Dan White's attorney.

Metcalf had just read *Orthomolecular Nutrition* by Abram Hoffer. He questioned Scherr about White's diet and learned that, while under stress, White would consume candy bars and soft drinks. Metcalf recommended the book to Scherr, suggesting the author as an expert witness. For, in his book, Hoffer revealed a personal vendetta against doughnuts, and White had once eaten five doughnuts in a row.

During the trial, psychiatrist Martin Blinder stated that, on the night before the murders, while White was "getting depressed about the fact he would not be reappointed [as supervisor], he just sat there in front of the TV set, bingeing on Twinkies." In my notebook, I scribbled "the Twinkie defense," and wrote about it in my next report.

In court, White just sat there in a state of complete

control bordering on catatonia, as he listened to an assembly line of psychiatrists tell the jury how out of control he had been. One even testified that, "If not for the aggravating fact of junk food, the homicides might not have taken place."

The Twinkie was invented in 1930 by James Dewar, who described it as "the best darn-tootin' idea I ever had." He got the idea of injecting little cakes with sugary cream-like filling and came up with the name while on a business trip, where he saw a billboard for Twinkle Toe Shoes. "I shortened it to make it a little zippier for the kids," he said.

In the wake of the Twinkie defense, a representative of the ITT-owned Continental Baking Company asserted that the notion that overdosing on the cream-filled goodies could lead to murderous behavior was "poppycock" and "crap"—apparently two of the artificial ingredients in Twinkies, along with sodium pyrophosphate and yellow dye—while another spokesperson for ITT couldn't believe "that a rational jury paid serious attention to that issue."

Nevertheless, some jurors did. One remarked after the trial that "It sounded like Dan White had hypoglycemia." Doug Schmidt's closing argument became almost an apologetic parody of his own defense. He told the jury that White did not have to be "slobbering at the mouth" to be subject to diminished capacity. Nor, he said, was this simply a case of "Eat a Twinkie and go crazy."

When Superior Court Judge Walter Calcagno presented the jury with his instructions, he assured them access to the evidence, except that they would not be allowed to have possession of White's gun and his ammunition at the same time. After all, these deliberations can get pretty heated. The judge was acting like a concerned schoolteacher offering Twinkies to students but withholding the cream filling to avoid any possible mess.

Each juror originally had to swear devotion to the criminal justice system. It was that very system that had allowed for a shrewd defense attorney's transmutation of a double political execution into the White Sugar Murders. On the walls of the city, graffiti cautioned, "Eat a Twinkie—Kill a Cop!"

In 1983, the *San Francisco Chronicle* published a correction: "In an article about Dan White's prison life, *Chronicle* writer Warren Hinckle reported that a friend of White expressed the former supervisor's displeasure with an article in the *San Francisco Bay Guardian* which made reference to the size of White's sexual organ. The *Chronicle* has since learned that the *Bay Guardian* did not publish any such article and we apologize for the error."

It was 10 feet long, 3 feet 6 inches high, 3 feet 8 inches wide, and weighed more than a ton—no, not Dan White's penis—the world's largest Twinkie, which was unveiled in Boston. And on the fiftieth anniversary of the Twinkie, inventor Dewar said, "Some people say Twinkies are the quintessential junk food, but I believe in the things. I fed them to my four kids, and they feed them to my fifteen grandchildren. Twinkies never hurt them."

◆ ◆ ◆

When the jurors walked into court to deliver the verdict, they appeared somber, except for a former cop, who smiled and triumphantly tapped the defense table twice with two fingers as he passed by, telegraphing the decision of voluntary manslaughter. White would be sentenced to seven years in prison.

In January 1984, he was paroled after serving a little more than five years. The estimated shelf life of a Twinkie is seven years. That's two years longer than White spent behind bars. When he was released, that Twinkie in his cupboard was still edible. But perhaps, instead of eating it, he would have it bronzed.

He called his old friend, Frank Falzon—the detective who had originally taken his confession—and they met.

"I hit him with the hard questions," Falzon recalled. "I asked him, 'What were those extra bullets for? What did happen?'"

"I really lost it that day," White replied.

"You can say that again," Falzon said.

"No. I really lost it. I was on a mission. I wanted four of them."

"Four?" Falzon asked.

"Carol Ruth Silver—she was the biggest snake of the bunch." (Silver realized that she might have been his third victim had she not stayed downstairs for a second cup of coffee that morning.) "And Willie Brown. He was master-minding the whole thing."

While White had been waiting to see Moscone in the anteroom of his office, the mayor was drinking coffee with Brown, chatting and laughing. Moscone told Brown that he had to see White, and Brown slipped out the back door just as Moscone was letting White in the front way. Thirty seconds later, White killed Moscone. The Marlboro cigarette in Moscone's hand would still be burning when the paramedics arrived.

White hurriedly walked across a long corridor to the

area where the supervisors' offices were. His name had already been removed from the door of his office, but he still had a key. He went inside and reloaded his gun. Then he walked out, past Supervisor Dianne Feinstein's office. She called to him, but he didn't stop. "I have to do something first," he told her, as he headed for Milk's office.

George Moscone's body was buried, and Harvey Milk's body was cremated. His ashes were placed in a box, which was wrapped in *Doonesbury* comic strips, then scattered at sea. The ashes had been mixed with bubble bath and two packets of grape Kool-Aid, forming a purple patch on the Pacific Ocean. Harvey would've liked that touch.

On the twenty-fifth anniversary of the twin assassination, the *San Francisco Chronicle* reported that, "During the trial, no one but well-known satirist Paul Krassner—who may have coined the phrase 'Twinkie defense'—played up that angle. His trial stories appeared in the *San Francisco Bay Guardian*. 'I don't think Twinkies were ever mentioned in testimony,' said chief defense attorney Douglas Schmidt, who recalls 'HoHos and Ding Dongs,' but no Twinkies." Apparently, he forgot that one of his own psychiatric witnesses, Martin Blinder, had used the T-word.

Blinder now complains, "If I found a cure for cancer, they'd still say I was the guy who invented 'the Twinkie defense.'"

The *Chronicle* also quoted Steven Scherr about the Twinkie defense: "'It drives me crazy,' said co-counsel Scherr, who suspects the simplistic explanation provides cover for those who want to minimize and trivialize what happened. If he ever strangles one of the people who says 'Twinkie defense' to him, Scherr said, it won't be because he's just eaten a Twinkie."

Scherr was sitting in the audience at the campus theater where a panel discussion of the case was taking place. I was one of the panelists. When Scherr was introduced from the stage, I couldn't resist saying to him on my microphone, "Care for a Twinkie?"

In October 1985, Dan White committed suicide by carbon monoxide poisoning in his garage. He taped a note to the windshield of his car, reading, "I'm sorry for all the pain and trouble I've caused."

I accept his apology. I got caught in the post-verdict riot and was beaten by a couple of cops. The injuries affected my posture and twisted my gait. I gradually developed an increasingly strange limp and I now walk with the aid of a cane. At the airport, I'm told by security to put my cane on the conveyor belt along with my overnight bag and my shoes, but then I'm handed an orange-colored wooden cane to enable me to walk through the metal detector.

You just never know what might be hidden inside a cane.

THE LAST ELECTION

The Republicans' party line that Barack Obama was "palling around with terrorists" didn't work, although some people believed it because then they wouldn't need a racist reason not to vote for Obama. Next, the campaign acted as though his advocacy of age-appropriate sex education for kindergarteners meant putting condoms on cucumbers. That didn't work, either. Then John McCain tried calling him a "socialist." Also didn't work. Ironically, Socialist Party candidate Norman Thomas ran for president six times, and never won, but every one of his platform planks were eventually adopted by Democrats and Republican administrations alike. They just didn't *call* it socialism.

In January 2009, Christian fundamentalist Pat Robertson stated that God told him America is headed for veritable socialism as well as an economic rebound under President-elect Obama. "What the Lord was saying," he claimed, "the people are willing to accept socialism to alleviate their pain. Cast off all the gloom and the doom because things are getting ready to turn around. I say with humility, I hope I've heard the Lord. I spend time praying and asking him for wisdom, and if there's a mistake, it's not his fault, it's mine." Humility in action.

In any case, one of the factors in Obama's win was indeed the confidence-destroying financial crisis, and now he faces a food chain of euphemisms. Hey, is this like the Great Depression? Nah, it's not a depression, it's only a recession. Wait, it's not a recession, it's just an economic downturn. No, it's not an economic downturn, it's a correction. Oops, it's not a corrrection, it's an adjustment. Hurry, get me a chiropractor. Similarly, there's a food-chain of solutions to the problem. From the Troubled Asset Relief Program to the Bailout Bill to the Rescue Package to the Emergency Economic Stability Act to Alan Greenspan confessing "My bad" to Free Botox for Everybody.

Perhaps the most bizarre byproduct of the campaign began with an anonymous ad on Craigslist headlined: "Need Sarah Palin Lookalike ASAP for Adult Film." The pay would be $3,000 and, it was duly noted, "No anal required." This porn flick, it turned out, would be shot by Hustler Video, and no, Tina Fey did not apply for the job. The climactic scene was a threesome with Sarah Palin, Condoleezza Rice and Hillary Clinton.

Hillary was played by veteran porn star and sex educator Nina Hartley, who told me that "The big hullabaloo over the movie is being generated by feminists from both the pro- and anti-porn sides. They're up in arms that 'women are being nonconsensually satirized' by Big Evil Porn and The Big Bad Larry Flynt. The usual nonsense from the usual suspects. Even some pro-porn feminists are upset at Palin being 'targeted' by Porn. They conveniently overlook the fact that most porn satirizes white men in power: politicians, police, professors. Most recent case in point, *The Elliot Splizter Story*. . . ."

Who's Nailin' Paylin was ready for release before the election, as was an issue of the horror comic book *Tales From the Crypt* that featured on the cover a painting of Sarah Palin swinging her hockey stick to disperse the Vault-Keeper and other ghoulish characters as she sneeringly asks, "Didn't we get rid of you guys in the '50s?"—a reference to the censorship problems faced decades ago by EC Comics, the original publisher of *Tales From the Crypt*, and concomitantly a criticism of Palin for her "rhetorical question" about removing objectionable books from library shelves.

However, another publisher was producing a comic-book biography of Palin that wouldn't be released until February 2009, so two endings were prepared. But an edition of *South Park*—broadcast the day after the election—took a risk with only one ending, which lampooned Obama's victory. Co-creator Trey Parker explained, "We're just going to make the Obama version, and if McCain somehow wins, we're basically just totally screwed." Likewise, Garry Trudeau gambled that Obama would win, and his syndicated *Doonesbury* strip—published the day after the election—depicted three soldiers in Iraq watching the returns on TV as a reporter is saying, "And it's official—Barack Obama has won."

Some editors were undecided about whether to publish it. Trudeau encouraged them to choose hope over fear. "If I'm wrong," he told the *Los Angeles Times*, "it'll be my face that'll be covered with eggs, not theirs." *Times* editors had decided, in the interest of accuracy, to wait for the election results, and if Obama won, they would publish the strip on Thursday, but then they must have realized it was just a comic strip, not investigative journalism, and they published it on Wednesday after all.

Trudeau thought that newspapers should run the strip because "polling data gives McCain a 3.7 percent chance of victory." Indeed, a week after Obama's win, McCain himself admitted to Jay Leno, "I can read the polls—they tried to keep 'em from me." There were dozens of polls, from ABC to Zogby, and, psychographic sophistication aside, they didn't always exactly agree. For example, in Nevada during the last week of October, one poll put Obama's lead at 12 percent, another at 7 percent, another at 5 percent and two others at 4 percent, which meant that, given the margin of sampling error, McCain could conceivably have been slightly ahead. This, then, was the last presidential election. In the future, you'll only need to vote for the pollster that you trust the most.

During the 1968 Democratic convention in Chicago, I was among 15,000 protesters who had gathered in Grant Park for a rally when the police, triggered by the actions of one of their own provocateurs, attacked the demonstrators and sadistically beat as many as they could reach. It seemed impossible that we could ever work within the system. But now, forty years later, there were 200,000 celebrants who had gathered in that same park, giddy with the excitement of Obama's victory. They had worked within the system. During the past four decades, there has been a linear progression from Jimi Hendrix playing "The Star-Spangled Banner" at Woodstock to Aretha Franklin singing "My Country, 'Tis of Thee" at the inauguration. Is it possible that this event signified the early tremors of a nonviolent revolution? As the late singer/songwriter Harry Chapin once said to me backstage at a benefit: "If you don't act like there's hope, there *is* no hope." And remember, placebos work. My main hope is that I won't be disappointed.

Meanwhile, the memorabilia business flourishes as millions of voters seek a variety of tangible items to remind them of the part they played in history simply by voting. You can find Obama's image or name on mouse pads, baby bibs, aprons, dog jerseys, bobbleheads, condoms, dildos, toilet paper, an ice-cream flavor (Ben & Jerry's "Yes Pecan"), niche buttons ("Ventriloquists for Obama") and T-shirts ("Now I Don't Have to Move to Canada").

Somebody bid $400 on eBay for the day-after-inauguration November 5, 2008 issue of the *New York Times*. *USA Today* printed 500,000 extra copies; the *Washington Post* printed 350,000 extras. The only thing I saved was a full-page ad by the 99 Cents Only Stores, which included a "Joe the Plumber Special" plunger. There was no limit on how many I could buy.

AND GOD SAID, "LET THERE BE FILF"

It was the film *Deep Throat* that first brought the language of porn into mainstream awareness. The Linda Lovelace character's clitoris was located deep in her throat, and the only way she could achieve orgasm was through oral sex. Years after that movie, *Washington Post* reporter Bob Woodward's secret source in the Watergate scandal, the late FBI agent W. Mark Felt, was given the code name "Deep Throat."

More recently, the acronym MILF has also entered mainstream awareness, in print, in films and on TV, from the hosts of fake news shows to sitcoms where the laugh track responds to hearing "She's a real MILF" uttered by a character, while parents try to avoid satisfying the curiosity of their kids by explaining that it means "Mothers I'd Like to Fuck."

Actually, the sentiment behind MILF is "The Wives of Other Guys I'd Like to Fuck," but TWOGILF sounds too much like a Dutch denomination of money. As a long-time strong supporter of equal rights, it occurred to me that there must also be a porn category called FILF. Likewise, even though it stands for "Fathers I'd Like to Fuck," it really signifies "The Husbands of Other Chicks I'd Like to Fuck," but THOCILF sounds too much like it could be a prescription medicine for vaginal dryness.

Please excuse my generalization—about wives rather than mothers, and husbands rather than fathers—because in my research of FILF on the Internet (there are 120,000 such listings), I came across a few where it signifies *other* sexual preferences. For example, there are those who believe that the first F in FILF "is definitely for Friends, not Fathers." Others insist that FILF applies to "Fatties I'd Like to Fuck." Many men are turned on by women who are obese.

FILF also applies to gays who prefer older guys, as in

"Fags I'd Like to Fuck." And did they think that the film MILK was an acronym for "Men I'd Like to Kiss"? One gay site states: "FILF (Fathers I'd Like to Fuck) is one of our favorite sections here at whatgaysite and we'll do anything to find you the best that's out there on the net. You just gotta love a hard-bodied daddyo with a throbbing cock hungry for fresh ass!"

And FILF can apply to teenage girls, such as the one who said, "Maybe he's one of our friend's Dads." A married male blogger wrote, "I won't say I'm thrilled with the dude who shouted 'MILF!' in *Baby Mama*, but I can certainly understand his point. Of course, this leaves unresolved the question of whether anyone has shouted 'FILF!' at me from a moving vehicle since a baby came into our lives. The answer is no. Not once have I been sexually harassed as a new father."

For women in their twenties and thirties, FILF represents handsome movie celebrities such as Brad Pitt, Matt Damon and Ben Affleck. One woman mentioned Ashton Kutcher, adding that "technically, he's only the stepdaddy." However, another woman made the connection between show biz and politics when she admitted, "Obama is hot. I wouldn't say no to him."

In fact, sex therapist Dr. Susan M. Block has featured "The Erotic Obama Fantasies Show" on her program, *Radio Suzy*. "The dashing young president is making numerous appearances in the erotic dreams and fantasies of many men and women of all races and ethnicities around the world," she said. "Certainly my own clients are having erotic fantasies about Barack Obama. One of my male clients said, 'I voted for Obama. I've got a black man in my White House, and now I want a black man in my white wife.' I've got clients who are fantasizing about him doing their wives."

A female listener called in and described her fantasy: "We're in the Oval Office. I'm wearing some sort of red presidential speech dress which is very elegant, and he's wearing that dark suit and tie, and I'm sort of ripping it off, so that the buttons are flying all over the Oval Office. And then I sort of bend over that Oval Office desk, and it's like, you know, a racist stereotype—he's very well hung. And I'm just doing the Lord's work. Serving my country."

If you type "Obama FILF" in the Google box, this question automatically pops up: "Did you mean Obama *film?*" There actually *is* a porn flick titled *Fathers I'd Like to Fuck*. Porn-film critic Roger Pipe points out in his review, "The idea of older guys fucking young chicks in porn isn't new. It isn't even a genre, really. It's just porn." But there has yet to be an anonymous ad on Craigslist for a Barack Obama lookalike.

Memo to Larry Flynt: "I'm patiently waiting for Hustler Video, the producers of *Who's Nailin' Paylin*, to come out with an appropriate sequel, titled *Pornobama*."

Yes, this president will finally become our FILF-in-Chief.

Paul Krassner's FBI files indicate that after *Life* magazine published a favorable profile of him, the FBI sent a poison-pen letter to the editor, complaining: "To classify Krassner as a social rebel is far too cute. He's a nut, a raving, unconfined nut." "The FBI was right," said George Carlin. "This man is dangerous—and funny, and necessary."

When *People* magazine called Krassner "father of the underground press," he immediately demanded a paternity test. He published the groundbreaking satirical magazine the *Realist* from 1958 to 1974, reincarnating it as a newsletter in 1985. "The taboos may have changed," he wrote, "but irreverence is still our only sacred cow." The final issue was published in Spring 2001.

His style of personal journalism constantly blurred the line between observer and participant. He interviewed a doctor who performed abortions when it was illegal, then ran an underground abortion referral service. He published material on the psychedelic revolution, then took LSD with Tim Leary, Ram Dass and Ken Kesey, later accompanying Groucho Marx on his first acid trip. He covered the antiwar movement, then co-founded the Yippies with Abbie Hoffman and Jerry Rubin (writing a few animated reenactment scenes for the documentary *Chicago 10* four decades later).

He edited Lenny Bruce's autobiography, *How to Talk Dirty and Influence People* and, with Lenny's encouragement, eventually became an award-winning stand-up comic himself, beginning at the Village Gate in 1961. Ten years later—five years after Lenny's death—Groucho said, "I predict that in time Paul Krassner will wind up as the only live Lenny Bruce." He was nominated for a 2005 Grammy

Award in the Album Notes category for his 5,000-word essay accompanying a 6-CD package, *Lenny Bruce: Let the Buyer Beware.*

Krassner's venues have ranged from the New Age Expo to the Skeptics Conference, from a Neo-Pagan Festival to the L.A. County Bar Association, from a Swingers Convention to the Brentwood Bakery, where members of the audience were each given a free pastry of their choice. Over the years, he has built up a cult following that has steadily been edging into mainstream awareness. The *New York Times:* "He is an expert at ferreting out hypocrisy and absurdism from the more solemn crannies of American culture." The *Los Angeles Times*: "He has the uncanny ability to alter your perceptions permanently." The *San Francisco Chronicle*: "Krassner is absolutely compelling. He has lived on the edge so long he gets his mail delivered there."

In 1980, he was head writer for an HBO special satirizing the presidential election campaign starring Ronald Reagan, and a decade later was a writer on Ron Reagan Jr.'s late-night TV talk show. He currently writes columns for *High Times* and *AVN* [Adult Video News] *Online*, and is an occasional contributor to *The Nation* and the *Los Angeles Times*. He is updating and expanding his autobiography, *Confessions of a Raving, Unconfined Nut: Misadventures in the Counterculture*, and working on his first novel.

Krassner is the only person in the world ever to win awards from both *Playboy* (for satire) and the Feminist Party Media Workshop (for journalism). He received an ACLU Uppie (Upton Sinclair) Award for dedication to freedom of expression. And at the Cannabis Cup in Amsterdam, he was inducted into the Counterculture Hall of Fame—"my ambition," he claims, "since I was three years old."